CREATIVE COUPLES

Books by Wallace Denton
Published by The Westminster Press

Family Problems and What to Do About Them
The Minister's Wife as a Counselor
What's Happening to Our Families?
The Role of the Minister's Wife

CREATIVE COUPLES
The Growth Factor in Marriage

WALLACE DENTON
JUANITA HOLT DENTON

THE WESTMINSTER PRESS
Philadelphia

©1983 Wallace Denton and Juanita Holt Denton

All rights reserved—no part of this book may be reproduced in any form without permission in writing from the publisher, except by a reviewer who wishes to quote brief passages in connection with a review in magazine or newspaper.

BOOK DESIGN BY ALICE DERR

First edition

Published by The Westminster Press®
Philadelphia, Pennsylvania

PRINTED IN THE UNITED STATES OF AMERICA
9   8   7   6   5   4   3   2   1

Library of Congress Cataloging in Publication Data

Denton, Wallace.
   Creative couples.

   Includes bibliographical references.
   1. Marriage. 2. Family. I. Denton, Juanita Holt, 1930–   . II. Title.
HQ734.D46 1983   646.7'8   82-17439
ISBN 0-664-24453-X (pbk.)

To
Pauline Oates
our Friend
who taught us the meaning
of Hospitality

Contents

Introduction 9

1. Growth Through Personal Identity 13
2. Portrait of Strong, Healthy Families 31
3. Enriching Your Sexual Relationship 51
4. Guidelines for Living with Children 68
5. Relating to the Other Generation 84
6. Friendship: Source of Personal
   and Family Strength 104
7. Building Family Memories—Family Rituals 123

Appendix: Questions and Exercises 139

Notes 149

Introduction

The capacity of the human brain for storing, analyzing, and retrieving data is so great that each of us, we are told, utilizes only a small fraction of its vast potential. That is, we have the intellectual power to soar like eagles, but too often grovel among weeds like serpents. This book is based on the belief that couples, like the brain, also have tremendous potential for growth which they never achieve. We have untapped possibilities for deeper intimacy, enriched communication, more joy in parenting, richer sexual relationships, and greater overall fulfillment than we ever experience. Instead, we often crawl among marital weeds.

Growth is a key concept in this book. To grow means we move toward achieving our potential for completeness, for wholeness. But growth requires change, and change makes some people most anxious. Others only want the mate to change ("If she'd just come to her senses!"). We now know that healthy, strong families are characterized by small but important changes taking place with regularity across the years as the family adapts to new circumstances. The older concept of marital success a few decades ago was a static one (unchanging) calling for "compatibility." Compatibility is needed in marriage, but we now know that yesterday's compatibility is today's incompatibility—unless there is growth in the relationship.

"You don't have to be sick to get better" is a slogan that was generated in the '60s. It is one of the better legacies left by that turbulent decade. It reminds us that our marriages, our families, do not have to be viewed as sick in order to be made better. This getting "better" is what we call growth. At the base of the marriage enrichment movement is a belief that despite the many problems besetting contemporary families, there are tens of thousands of strong, healthy marriages in this country, and a conviction that growth will keep them that way. Marriage enrichment is for strong families; you cannot enrich something that does not already possess richness. This book is for these strong families who want to keep growing.

We are indebted to those who have helped make this book possible: to Charleen Carmony, who typed the final manuscript; to Purdue University for granting Wallace a sabbatical leave to work on the book; to the Southern Baptist Theological Seminary for letting us live and work on its campus during the writing; to our children, who permitted us to invade the privacy of their lives by sharing our experiences with them in these pages. Wayne and his wife, Susan, and our daughter, Susan, and her husband, Don, have taught us much of what we know about families.

We trust that this volume will be of use to couples, and groups of couples, interested in enriching their marriages. (To facilitate thought and discussion, questions and exercises are included for each chapter in the Appendix.) It is written with the hope that it will help your strong, healthy family to grow even stronger, healthier, and the bonds between you more satisfying. Remember: You don't have to have a sick family for it to be made better!

> There is nothing stronger
> and nobler than when man and wife
> are of one heart and mind in a house,
> A grief to their foes,
> and to their friends great joy,
> but their own hearts know it best.
> > Homer (ninth century B.C.)

W.D.
J.H.D.

1
Growth Through Personal Identity

We begin this book on couples and families by focusing on the individual. This may strike you as strange. However, we do so because of a conviction that there can be no growing couples and families apart from growing individuals. A vital part of personal growth has to do with one's sense of personal identity: Who am I? What am I like? How do I feel about being female (male)? How competent am I? How worthwhile am I? How comfortable am I with myself? Questions related to one's identity could go on and on. We believe that a clear, integrating, healthy sense of identity is necessary to being a satisfying and intimate marital partner. In fact, if Erik Erikson is right, the development of one's identity precedes the ability to be truly intimate.[1]

Rather than write a more "academic" chapter on personal identity and growth, we thought it might facilitate exploration of these dimensions in your life if we shared ourselves with you more personally in these areas. Accordingly, we have decided that in this chapter each of us will separately examine marriage and the family through the lens of our own experience in life and the ways this has affected our growth and identity. Wallace will share his "story" first, and this will be followed by Juanita's. (Among primitive peoples, the storyteller is one of the most important persons in the community. He is the repository of the group's past victories, defeats, disasters, heroes. The recounting of the group's "story" is a time calling forth both solemnity and celebration for those who listen. In a realistic sense, the group is bound together by its story. We use the concept of story here in much the same sense. It is our story that largely imparts to us a sense of identity as individuals; our story together as husband and wife serves to bond us as a couple. Your story serves the same function for you.)

WALLACE'S STORY

My initial reaction to writing this part of the book was wondering what to say. Personal statements I have read by other authors are usually full of conflict, drama, struggle, doubt, and perhaps a few sexual affairs thrown in for good measure. As I reflect on my life, I see that it has been characterized by relatively little conflict, struggle, doubt, and no affairs! (This confession will doubtless comfort my wife, but disappoint readers hoping for a tale of intrigue and passion.) I have always seemed to know who I am and where I am going. Once a decision is made, I usually manage to convince myself that whatever I have done is best. (The only important decisions I have regretted involved automobiles. I have had several "affairs" with cars!) All of this sounds rather dull, doesn't it? Perhaps even egotistical.

However, those are my initial reactions. As I look more closely, I discern struggles, conflicts, and doubts that are not immediately apparent. (The closer look afforded by the microscope always brings into view hidden worlds which the unaided eye cannot discover.) For instance, I recall with discomfort our first few years of marriage when I was so young, so inexperienced, so insecure in my new role as man and husband. If while I was driving Juanita said, "Watch out for that car!", that was experienced by me not only as a criticism of my driving but as an assault upon my competence as a man as well. This provoked many angry outbreaks on my part. I recall angrily informing her one day that I wanted her to sit silently and pretend she was a passenger on a Greyhound bus! There are two realities here: First, she doubtless kept me from having a few wrecks. The second is that my fragile ego could not at that time handle even such gentle jolting as a traffic warning from my wife.

All of this reminds me that I find men to be strange creatures of contradictions. We strut and posture and flex our muscles, yet the typical masculine ego is so delicate, so fragile. Like a moth, it can hardly be handled without damage. So we men protect that fragile entity with bravado, or threats, or outbursts of anger which (perhaps unconsciously) are designed to intimidate family members into silence. Our sense of authority, of power, is so easily challenged that even the slightest question from our wives is often perceived as a full attack on those symbols of masculinity—authority, power. I think the word "power" is a key to understanding men. We seem to *have* to have power. This isn't just confined to the Western world. In many cultures men perform secret rites, chant secret songs, sometimes in special buildings from which women are excluded. Why? I think it is because all of this gives them power—power that women do not have! Even the word used to describe a phenomenon that evokes fear in men second only to cancer, according to one study, is "impotence." It means "without power." Call a man a rogue, a scoundrel, or a maverick and he can live with these. He may even be proud of the labels. But don't call him weak, especially if he isn't too sure. "Weak" is the deepest cut of all.

But I suspect that most men are not aware of how fragile their ego is. Of course, women have known for eons. Because of this, wives have played dumb over the centuries, or kept their mouths shut even when we were dead wrong and about to make fools of ourselves—or have an auto accident! Some have agreed with their husbands rather than risk wounding their ego and precipitate an angry outbreak. But more often women have become subtle manipulators of men. Some call it "diplomacy," which can be defined as the art of letting your husband have your way. (This, in part, explains the popularity of such books as Marabel Morgan's *Total Woman*, which we view as an excellent document on how to manipulate a husband. The secret to the manipulation is to ply him with sex and make him feel like a king!)

As I reflect on my own sense of identity as a man and a husband, I am forced to examine my roots—my story. My family of origin and the culture in which it was nested have inevitably influenced (but not determined) who I am and have been in these areas. My personal odyssey began in the back bedroom of a small house in Imperial Valley, California. My father could barely afford to pay the doctor attending his first child's birth, much less handle the additional expense of a hospital. He had fled Arkansas as a teenager seeking his fortune in the "promised land" of California. But, like so many other refugees from the South, he discovered only hard work and no fortune. He used to say that after eighteen years, all he had to show for it was a wife and four kids. (This bothered me a little, since I wasn't sure whether he was disappointed by the absence of the fortune or the presence of four kids!)

When I was fourteen, he packed his worldly possessions

in a four-wheel trailer made from a Model T Ford and began a new life in Arkansas in the same community in which he was born and reared. We spent the next several years sharecropping (i.e., giving the landowner a share of the crop instead of cash rent). Only after I was in college was he able to purchase a small farm.

During my years in Arkansas, we lived at the survival level, doing subsistence farming, raising a little cotton, cattle, and corn. The corn was fed to the cattle and the mules with which we farmed. Seldom was any sold. Cash came from the cotton and the cattle. There was no electricity (nor had we had any in California), water came from a hand-dug well, and the plumbing consisted of washtubs and a path. Our main contact with the outside world came through the radio powered by an auto battery, which was played sparingly. There was no newspaper, but our better-to-do relatives in Hot Springs brought us the old *Reader's Digest*s, which I read avidly. However, it must be emphasized that I did not feel deprived, since no one I knew lived any differently, and I felt accepted by my family and friends. It was a happy and exciting life.

The models of masculinity that I found in my father and other men in our circle of relatives and friends were rather consistent, calling for clear-cut role expectations for both men and women. A man, a real man, was honest and independent; he worked hard, paid cash, took care of his family, protected his wife's and children's honor, liked to hunt. A real man was a good, steady worker. To be accused of being lazy was worse than being called a scoundrel. A man was faithful to his wife and enjoyed his children. A man, a real man, was physically strong. Bulging muscles were an important validation of that masculinity.

In the world in which I grew up, a man's skill in fighting and willingness to fight were important. (No dirty fighting, just plain slugging it out.) As a matter of fact, fights among adult men were rare, but a man needed to communicate a tough readiness to fight should honor and necessity call for it. I remember my father proudly reciting the fights he had as a boy. One of my earliest memories is of him sparring with me, teaching me how to fight, making "a man" out of me. Yet somehow fighting was never really in me, and as I got older I began to question why it was important. But I was a child of my day, and as an adolescent, worked on developing my muscles by faithfully lifting a piece of railroad rail and developing my grip using advice I got from a muscle-building uncle. Alas, the muscles did not develop on me as they did on either the uncle or my father!

I worked alongside my father in the summers from the time I was eleven and he made his living baling hay in California. By the time I was thirteen, I was doing a man's work. Again, this was not unusual in our social circles. In fact, after we moved to Arkansas, the whole family went to the field. The modern, urban boy knows more about his mother's world than his father's, which is off in a plant or office across town. I suspect this in some way handicaps the modern boy in identifying with his father's role and coming to think of himself as a man.

The model of manliness set for me by my father in addition to hard work was one that included a lot of touching and verbal expression of love and affection. A man could be gentle and affectionate within the family without being considered weak or mushy. However, there was little touching outside the family. Perhaps this accounts for my being much the same way.

All of the above is not particularly important except to show some of the influences that have helped shape my identity. The role models of husband and man held up for me to emulate were in most respects quite traditional, even macho, and role expectations were clear. There is nothing necessarily wrong with such models, since they served the men and women in that culture quite well. Such models do not serve me or my son so well in the world in which we now live.

All of this has influenced the kind of husband and man I am and have been. It helped to make me irritable when Juanita warned me of a possible traffic hazard. It challenged my competence as a driver. My mother didn't do that with my father. My background also meant that I was honor-bound after marriage to pay our full educational expenses for the eight years we were in school. I grew up on a philosophy that if a man was old enough to marry, he was old enough to support himself and his family. So I neither asked for financial help (which sometimes was much needed), nor received any. But my father did well to take care of the rest of the family; he had no financial help to offer. However, had he offered it, my sense of pride as a self-sufficient and independent man would not have permitted me to take it.

One of the strange things that I sometimes ponder is why I am not more like the models of masculinity of the world in which I grew up. Education doubtless has something to do with this. Perhaps there was some unconscious agreement in the family that I was to work with my mind. One of my early memories is of both my mother and my father saying they wanted me to get a good education so that, as my father put it, "You don't have to work for a living like I have." (Unless you work and sweat like a mule, my father still doesn't consider it work!)

Religion was an important dimension of our family's life. At sixteen I decided to become a minister, after a minister took a special interest in our family. He was the most important person in the community and the most important person I knew. (My identification with him in my career choice is apparent.) So it was a few months later, at the tender age of sixteen, my family proudly sent me off to college, the first one on either side of the family to go to college. I arrived in that utterly alien world a country kid who had never been to a barbershop for a haircut, and with a supply of bed sheets made from cloth fertilizer sacks my mother had bleached and sewed together.

At this point in life I began to feel different in ways that bothered me. Whereas before, everyone I knew dressed and lived much like my family, now my backwardness and social awkwardness became apparent as I associated with fellow students from "the big cities." (Unknown to me was the fact that many of them were out of backgrounds similar to mine.) While my feelings of inadequacy and inferiority were not incapacitating, I was keenly aware of them. My dress, my hair, my language was that of a rough, unpolished, unsophisticated backwoodsman. One night friends playfully took me down and forcibly cut my hair, which was long by their standards. They meant no harm, but I remember the incident vividly. Still, in all of this I had a clear sense of direction—God had called me to be a minister. There was no wavering in that conviction. However, outside that role, I did not have much identity that I then trusted or with which I was comfortable. I certainly had no pride in being a country boy. I was not comfortable with my "story" at that point in life. I *needed* the role of minister. It gave me an identity I otherwise lacked. But perhaps this is to be expected of teenagers, most of whom have shaky identities.

The first week of my senior year in college I surveyed the new crop of freshman women arriving on campus when one in particular caught my eye. Through my roommate, I found that her name was Juanita and that she was a competent, accomplished person in several areas. I was somewhat intimidated by the fact that she was a sophisticated "big city" girl. (I was to discover later that her parents were no more sophisticated than mine.) On our campus she was promptly elected editor of the college paper (a position she had also held in high school), and played first-chair trombone in the marching band. (However, her marching skills were strictly "last chair" caliber!) Though I liked her a lot, I was not sure whether a sophisticated lady would be interested in an unsophisticated guy. To make a long story short, to my surprise, she was interested, and nearly two years later we were married.

Three persons outside my family have been the primary influences in my life, persons who believed in me, helped me to dream dreams I never dreamed of dreaming, and supported me in fulfilling those dreams. The first, pivotal person was that self-educated country preacher, H. S. Coleman, who took an interest in me and got me enrolled in college. Without his encouragement, I might today be an uneducated, itinerant country preacher like so many of the role models I had in our corner of the world. The second pivotal person is Juanita. She is the "Special Woman" in my life whom Daniel Levinson says so many men have.[2] She, too, has helped me to dream and fulfill dreams. She is an open, straightforward communicator who relates with no "games." She has helped me to be the "up front" communicator in the family. Though she has brought far more joy to my life than anyone else, she also clearly heads the list of being at times the person who presses me to the outer limits of my self-control and I explode in angry rage! Part of the reason for this is that she cannot be intimidated or cowed by my best machinations. She has a bright mind, an absolutely indomitable spirit, and a clear sense of her own identity and worth. She was a liberated woman before we had a term for it!

The third pivotal person is Wayne E. Oates. When I first came to know him, he was a young professor at the Southern Baptist Seminary in Louisville doing pioneering work in the emerging field of psychology of religion and pastoral care. Through him I was introduced to the field of the family and family therapy. He encouraged me to apply for an internship in family therapy at Merrill-Palmer Institute, and then for doctoral work at Columbia University. Until then, never in my wildest dreams had I ever thought of getting a doctorate. Only the brilliant, I thought, got doctorates. (I did not realize that it mainly takes a modicum of intelligence, and a generous helping of tenacity!) That this man, who stood so very tall in my estimation, believed in and saw something worth developing in me, and became my mentor, was most affirming.

Others have also made important contributions to my life, such as Aaron Rutledge at Merrill-Palmer Institute, and Ernest Osborne at Columbia University. It would take another chapter to trace the development of my identity across the years to becoming a member of Purdue University's faculty. Suffice it to say that for me it has all been a part of a continuous and clear sense of direction and identity as I moved from one stage of life to the next. This sense of direction and identity has imparted a substantial measure of stability to my life. With the passing of the years, as I have become more integrated and comfortable within myself, I have been able to go back and appreciate and affirm those positive dimensions of my story that have helped to shape and mold me. But scratch the surface of this professor, and you will still find a backwoodsman. But I like that!

As I examine my story, I am aware that I am a husband, father, man much like those in the world in which I grew up; yet, in important ways I am also very different from them. Cultural influence is not predestination. Because of this, we can choose to be different from some aspects of our cultural background. Our son and daughter, too, will affirm some dimensions of the heritage Juanita and I have provided, but they will also have clear ideas about ways and areas in which they want to be and do things differently. This is as it should be. In this way, they work out their own identities, just as we have worked out ours. They will have to integrate and make peace with their "story" just as we have had to integrate and make peace with ours.

Juanita's Story

In this book, Wallace and I attempt to look at growth as it affects couples and their families from several vantage points. There is also an emphasis that before we can grow as "we," there must be growth as "me." Especially there is concern for the "me" within the pair relationship, and the ways each of us as individuals gives shape to the marriage context in which we experience our lives.

I now come to the part of the chapter where I attempt to make a personal statement concerning my own identity and experience with life. This is not an easy task. To write about "me," to give recognition to where I began and where I am, and to be sensitive to this as it appears from my personal awareness as a woman, requires a risk. However, risk is always necessary to growth.

First, I am preparing to risk in this chapter that you, the reader, will accept this as one person's struggle to tell her story. Before I could tell it, I had to learn to value my story. I also learned to trust it. Trusting it is important so that when you tell me your story, I will not think there is something wrong with mine. After all, my story is me; your story is you! This has helped me when I have heard so many voices crying in the wilderness with conflicting stories of where I am to look to find my "me."

Where does my story begin?

I believe that as I try to put the pieces of my story together, I do not have to be in touch with every single piece. When I look at the parts of my story, there are some things that are more significant to my marriage and family relationships than others. These are the pieces that I choose to explore here.

For a beginning, it might be significant to be aware of the fact that I made my entrance into the world in a small apartment in the back of an Arkansas grocery store, owned by my parents. Since these were years of the Great Depression, uncollected bills from customers piled so high that my parents were forced out of business. This information is important, because it dates me! I grew up in a world where security was threatened, and survival needs were more important than "growth as persons."

However, I was touched by much more during these early years than survival needs. An awareness of this is significant as I relate to those about me, and important to my story. For one thing, from age three to eight, I lived in a house far out in the Arkansas countryside. Our family moved there, after nearly three years of work trying to survive in the Texas oil fields. In this primitive country house, neighbors were distant, relatives lived across the state, and visiting with the clan was quite infrequent. My only sibling, a brother, five years older than I, was gone each weekday to school in a nearby town.

My days during this period of my life were filled with a great deal of aloneness. Having a playmate, other than my brother, was rare. My main activity before starting to school was roaming through the woods around our house with a dog my father kept for hunting. The only book I remember us having was *Robinson Crusoe*, and when my brother returned from school, I got him to read this to me over and over again.

Why is this information important to understanding my growth as a person, my marriage, and other relationships? I must first of all come to terms with what solitude means to me. I would perhaps have to continue to deal with those early ways I learned to, or not to, communicate with another. The impact that *Robinson Crusoe* had on my life might explain the fascination I have had with the development of one's inner resources. Even my longing for a "Friday," a friend, may have found its early rootage here.

At the age of eight we moved from the country. Until I graduated from high school, most of my years were spent in an Arkansas town richly influenced by an oil boom. Oil money helped develop the community culturally and greatly improved the quality of public education. Churches, too, were better able to provide a wider range of ministries. This environment, I believe, had a significant influence on my development as a person. I was especially influenced those years by many people in an enlightened church community, which was like a second home to me.

I do not want to give the impression that a community filled with "new and quick money" is a simple one. In fact, at times it presented complex situations. There were those who lived in poverty one year, discovered oil on their land the next, and were wealthy by the following year. For those, like myself, who grew up in homes where finances were limited, we were constantly being confronted with what "sudden" money could do for our classmates. I think it made me all the more determined "to make it—in spite of being poor!" While in high school, I began to build an intense philosophy (or maybe a defense at the time) not to be impressed by wealth—for the sake of wealth alone. I believe this has continued to help give shape to my personal values to this day.

Up to this point, I have identified myself as a person with a world history (the Depression, etc.); a young child with a personal history (much solitude but early opportunities for introspection); an adolescent living in a particular kind of community (exposed to many cultural advantages, even though survival was an important goal in my own family); and a member of an enlightened church that helped me to develop a healthy religious faith (even though I was later severely tested with the religious doubts of a growing adolescent). With all of this as part of my baggage, I was a university student of the '50s, definitely a part of my culture, but also a young woman with a desire for a personal adventure with my "unique me."

Not many women of my generation completed college, only around ten percent. And those of us who attended were confronted with the "coattail philosophy" of being a woman, who would eventually be a wife. That is: Woman is known by the man she marries. Later, when the man becomes committed to investing most of his energy finding his "me" in his work world, then woman will also be known by her children. I have never completely bought that philosophy, especially if marriage means a woman is no longer responsible for the uniqueness of her own personal growth. However, because I became a full-time homemaker after our children were born, it may have appeared that I did. But I'm getting ahead of myself.

Between my sophomore and junior years in college, I married. Beyond the marriage though, even with great financial pressures (but with complete emotional and financial support from Wallace), I finished the university, then received a Master of Religious Education degree, and completed a graduate program in human development at the Merrill-Palmer Institute in Detroit before our first child was born. When I married, everyone was saying, "She will never finish school; she will have a baby the first year." Six years later they were saying, "She will never have a baby; she will go to school forever!"

Our baby came "in our own time." Making choices about the children in our marriage (we have two) has always been important to me. It is one part of my story that I especially think has significance. One of these choices was that during the child-rearing years, as long as we were financially able I would spend my primary "professional" interests and time in the home. Because of great professional demands in Wallace's work, and the high value we both place on our family, this decision for us seemed to be the best one. We felt our family needed a "full-time administrator." I have never regretted this choice.

There are many choices I have made in life which may not always have been the best ones. Nonetheless, they were my choices made within the context of the best thinking I had at the time. More important for me is the fact that I am willing to assume responsibility for these choices. Why is assuming responsibility for my choices important? Partly because I do not choose to spend a great deal of emotional energy regretting decisions that are now history. I see nothing creative in nursing regrets for not writing chapters in my story other than the ones I wrote. It is important to my continuing "me" that I accept the context of where I am, for better or worse, and move my story forward to the next chapter. I cannot identify with those who are embittered by what life "took from them" or decisons they made which they now regret. I choose to devote my time to dealing with chapters yet to be written. Grandma was right when she said, "What good is there in crying over spilt milk?"

A woman who chooses to devote her primary energies to the home does not have to "look into the diaper pail" as her main source of inspiration. I discovered, during these child-rearing years, several significant things for my personal growth. First of all, I located the public library. It became a way of life for me and the children to make pilgrimages to this shrine of the open door to a larger world. I also became a professional volunteer. (Time is more flexible in this role.) I discovered that when I took a volunteer position seriously, working at it with the same expertise and commitment of a paid position, others treated me professionally. I was amused and flattered by occasionally being introduced as "Dr. Juanita Denton" and sometimes labeled a Purdue professor, when my briefcase was really a diaper bag. (Incidentally, a diaper bag is now my briefcase.)

This professional attitude toward volunteer activities was important to me because later when I entered "the work world" as a full-time salaried professional, I felt no real gap of insecurity. Naturally, I did not immediately become the top paid person where I was employed. However, since I was now middle-aged, my values about what was "top" had changed.

Another way I chose to continue my personal growth during the child-rearing years was by continuing my education. Even though our son was an infant, I remained a part-time student at Columbia University and Union Theological Seminary while Wallace worked on his doctorate. This was for me my "art class" or "sewing club" which others, more talented in these areas than I, used for their personal growth and self-expression.

When we moved to Lafayette, Indiana, eighteen years ago, I again became a part-time student. By taking one or two courses a semester, I completed a second master's degree at Purdue University. Following this, I enrolled in a graduate program in counseling and completed requirements for state certification in that area. Also, during this time I began investing a limited amount of time in a private counseling practice, participated as a leader in marriage and family enrichment workshops, and wrote articles for publication in this field. (Later, time permitted me to expand this part of my life even more, in addition to accepting a full-time position of employment.)

I hope that my appreciation for my own growth as a person has been as significant for my family as it has been for me. I never felt that Wallace pushed me in any direction, though some wives report feeling pushed by their husbands. He supported me but did not either push or smother me. (There have been times I have thought he could have encouraged me more. But, when I am honest, I would have to admit I probably would have interpreted it as "pushing.")

Most of what I have written in this chapter has addressed my concerns toward the task of being wife-mother-career person. I chose to write about this to show how one person met this challenge, because I believe this is of great concern to many women. Fortunately, there are many good role models available to women today. And even better, they present a wide variety of ways to reach the desired goals for family living.

There are many other pieces of my story I have left out. Friends have played a vital role in my development as a person. Fortunately, we have a chapter on friendship later in the book. Space also does not permit exploration of what life has taught me about commitments, or how I have found in my personal religious faith limitless paths for growth. Nor have I dealt with the intense emotional pain that was mine as growth required me to move from one stage to another. Suffice it to say, there were many days I felt lost, bored, anxious, and fragmented. Women readers, in particular, perhaps know what I mean.

It would also require considerable space for Wallace and me to describe adequately the dimensions of personhood cultivated in our lives by our children. Our son, now in a psychiatry residency, and our daughter, a landscape architect, challenged all that we were and knew in their days of childhood and adolescence. They expanded our horizons, exasperated our depths, brought us unlimited joy, tested our fortitude, and all in all, for better or worse, helped to make us both more of what we are today.

In conclusion, even though we could not cover everything, one of the goals we had in writing this chapter is to help you to have some grasp of us as persons as you read the book. We also hope that in risking sharing a little of our pilgrimages in life, you have been stimulated to explore your own pilgrimage and come to appreciate your story, your relationships, your commitments. Perhaps, like us, there are parts of your story that you wish were different. These may be having a negative impact on your marriage. In this case, we hope that you will see that regardless of what has happened in the past, you can *choose* to make the most of chapters yet to be written in your life. You can choose to be a growing couple. To be sure, this may be painful. While pain does not necessarily produce growth, we are firmly convinced that without pain there is no personal growth or growth as a couple. We hope that the following pages will help you in writing chapters yet to be lived in ways that will be rewarding both personally and as a family.

2
Portrait of Strong, Healthy Families

Nathaniel Hawthorne's short story "The Great Stone Face" traces the life of a boy growing up in the shadow of a great stone face etched in profile on a mountainside by the forces of nature. He loved that mountain and grew into manhood under the overarching influence of its presence. Legend had it that one day a great and wise man would be born in their valley who would look like that stone face, and he hoped to live long enough to meet the great man. Then one day many years later, that boy, now a mature man, spoke to a crowd with great eloquence and wisdom, when someone was startled to notice that he had over the years inexplicably come to look just like the great stone face!

We like that story, for it is a commentary on the influence of a model. Its message is that we tend to become like the models whom we admire and respect. Can it be that one reason we do not have more strong, healthy families is that we have not had good role models to follow? Perhaps our models have been outdated and distorted, so that it is difficult to identify with them. On the other hand, some contemporary models, while perhaps superficially appealing, are ultimately self-defeating because they lack commitment to anything more substantial than "do your own thing." We believe some of the current research now being conducted on strong, healthy families is providing a remedy to this situation by aiding us in understanding what contemporary healthy families are like. Perhaps these are the models we need in today's world.

In this chapter we will explore the nature of some of these healthy families. It will be perhaps a bit more "academic" than other chapters, but we view it as foundational to much of what will follow in subsequent chapters. We think you will find some of the qualities characterizing strong families to be exciting. In them you will discover the strengths in your own family, and find clues to ways in which you can make your own family stronger. This becoming stronger, or growing as families, is the theme of this entire book.

Almost from the beginning of the study of the family in the 1920s, family specialists have attempted to understand what strong, healthy, functional families are like by studying weak, sick, dysfunctional families. Strange! This focus on pathology led Abraham Maslow to accuse his fellow psychologists of having a "sick psychology." Sigmund Freud, he said, had given us the sick half of psychology and "we must now fill it out with the healthy half."[3] We have also had a "sick family" orientation. This is changing now as we add the "healthy half" to family studies.

We think the most exciting area of family study in recent years has been that research into the nature of healthy, strong families by examining what healthy, strong families, not sick ones, are like. We believe this research can provide a model for contemporary growing families. Perhaps these can serve as a kind of road map for guiding younger couples in establishing their own families.

Toward Defining Strong, Healthy Families

A major problem which family specialists have confronted is that of defining what healthy families are like. Despite the difficulty of their task, family specialists have made significant progress in agreeing on the basic characteristics of strong, healthy families. But some definition of terms is necessary and we begin by looking at two terms often associated with the subject—"normal" and "healthy."

Sometimes the terms "normal" and "healthy" are used interchangeably. However, some authors maintain that the terms should be assigned separate meanings. Donald Price asserts that "normal" should be reserved "exclusively for speaking of the statistical average, generally the majority or typical behavior."[4] We agree. The normal husband or wife, as computed by statistical averages, may at some time in life be unfaithful to the marriage vows, but such "normalcy" can hardly be considered healthy to the marital relationship. And the normal family may be too deeply in debt, but this statistical average can hardly be considered healthy. On the other hand, we believe the term "healthy" should be reserved, as John S. Sennott suggests, to describe "optimal functioning as determined by a theoretical system."[5] We will use the term in that sense mainly following the theoretical system of the Circumplex Model described below.

We will be using the terms "healthy," "strong," and "functional" interchangeably. An examination of the literature reveals a number of other adjectives used to describe this type of family. Among these are: balanced, competent, effective, excellent, successful, fully functioning, superior, growth-oriented, and nurturing. We prefer to speak of strong, healthy, or functional families. In speaking of health, we are reminded of the fact that the words health, holy, hale, and whole all come from the same root word meaning to be complete. Thus, we might say that healthy families are whole, complete.

THE CIRCUMPLEX MODEL OF HEALTHY FAMILY FUNCTIONING

In our judgement, the most significant work conceptualizing healthy family functioning is that of David Olson, Douglas Sprenkle, and Candyce Russell (called the Circumplex Model) and presented in several journal articles.[6] Because it is so basic to the topic under discussion here, we want to review this research. In brief, these family specialists believe that family health is dependent upon the proper balance of three basic dimensions of family life: their *cohesion*, their *adaptability*, and their *communication*. Let us briefly examine each one of these.

Cohesion refers to the emotional ties that family members have to each other and the degree to which each person in the family is free to be himself or herself. Cohesion can be conceived of as existing along a continuum thusly:

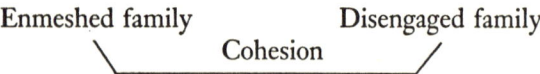

When cohesion is taken to one extreme, there is a family that is said to be *enmeshed*. That is, family members are too involved, too bonded together, so that there is little or no room for individuality, for differentness, for self-identity. This is a deceptive form of family dysfunction, since at first glance they appear to embody the Ideal American Family.

They do everything together. They are togetherness personified. They may seldom do things with other families. If family members have "bought into" this way of doing things, this ideal image is further enhanced by a relative absence of quarreling. They appear to be one big happy family, but sooner or later, the pressures for conformity begin to tell and fractures appear in the facade of the Ideal American Family because differentness is not tolerated and one or more members may have trouble continuing to think and be like everyone else.

How does a child (or other family member) cope with the smothery togetherness of an enmeshed family? One option is to capitulate and simply go along with the family and become a part of what Murray Bowen calls an "undifferentiated ego mass." We are all acquainted with these children who even as adults often fail to pull away from the family and establish their own identities. In those "super nice" enmeshed families, it is most difficult for a teenage or adult child to pull back from the family to establish a separate identity because of feeling so guilty hurting such wonderful parents—and they *will* be hurt, since they view pulling back as rejection. Another option is to rebel and rip away from the family by doing something such as running away.

On the other end of the continuum is a family that is just the opposite—*disengaged*. That is, family members have too little cohesion, not enough sense of belonging. In this kind of family the members have few emotional ties to each other and little sense of family identity and loyalty.

How does a child cope with being a part of a disengaged family? Since there is so little sense of "familyness" here it is difficult to feel a sense of belonging. Everybody is too busy doing his or her own thing. The child may attempt to get parental attention by rebelling and getting into trouble (sex, drugs, etc.). Or the son or daughter may run away and find a circle of people in which he or she feels a sense of belonging. Strange and radical groups are full of young people like this.

The authors of the Circumplex Model believe that the healthiest families avoid both extremes of cohesion and strike a balance between too much cohesion (enmeshment) and too little (disengagement).

Adaptability refers to the ability of a family to be flexible, to change the ways the members relate to each other as circumstances change, i.e., as parents and children grow older, or as stress and conflict indicate a need for change. Healthy families can make changes; dysfunctional families cannot or have difficulty making changes. Again, adaptability can be conceived of along a continuum:

Chaotic family   Rigid family
　　　　　　　　Adaptability

A *chaotic family* is so flexible, so devoid of structure and rules, that utter chaos reigns. At the other extreme, a *rigid family* has so much structure, so many rules, is so devoid of flexibility that it becomes sick because of its inability to make necessary changes.

A child growing up in a chaotic family is usually undisciplined, has trouble relating to authority, trouble following even necessary rules, is often angry, and very anxious and uncertain of himself or herself. Such a child may go through life this way, or during the teen years may seek structure and discipline by joining a group led by an autocratic, dictatorial figure as is often seen in some religious cults.

A child growing up in a family at the other extreme, a rigid family, may simply capitulate and go along with the family. This person seems incapable of thinking for himself or herself. Or this child may rebel and "break the parent's heart" or perhaps run away from home in an attempt to express an individuality which the rigid home does not permit. Thinking differently, being different in a rigid home is viewed as dangerous and wrong. (This may appear to be much like the description of the rebelling enmeshed child. However, the rebelling may be the same, but the reasons for doing it are different.)

As with cohesion, it appears that the healthiest, most functional families avoid either extreme in adaptability and strike a balance somewhere between chaos and rigidity.

Communication is defined as the giving and receiving of information. It is the transferring of an idea from one mind to another. This can be done through words, gestures, voice inflection, or one of several other means.

Unlike cohesion and adaptability, the authors of the Circumplex Model think that a high level, rather than moderate, of communication characterizes healthy, functional families. However, we agree with Michael Warner, who asserts that a balance in communication is as important as in the other two variables of cohesion and adaptability.[7] That is, communication can also be viewed as existing along a continuum:

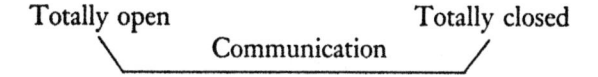

```
Totally open                    Totally closed
       \         Communication         /
```

If we conceive of one extreme of communication as being total openness, complete communication of every thought, feeling, desire, and the other end of the continuum representing the total absence of communicating these thoughts, feelings, desires, then perhaps a balance between these two extremes is desirable. (We suspect, however, that the authors of the Circumplex Model did not have total openness in mind when supporting a "high level" of communication.) One thing that sometimes plagues a marriage is a husband or a wife who under the banner of honesty and openness insists on sharing with the mate every thought, feeling, or desire. Thus, one wife insisted on sharing with her husband every negative feeling she had about his family under the guise of openness. Another husband shared with his wife ("because I'm honest") his many fantasies about the women at work. Needless to say, such openness had a devastating effect on those two marriages. One of the finest ways we know to be cruel and vicious is to be totally open.

We believe open communication should take place when knowledge of what is shared is necessary to the growth or continued smooth functioning of the relationship. This means that some things are best kept to oneself because the other person does not need to know of them. But it also means that some things must be shared with the mate, painful though they may be, because without that knowledge, the relationship cannot grow. Thus, the husband with the fantasies does not need to share these with his wife, but he does need to talk with her about their sexual relationship, if that is an issue.

These, then, are the basic tenets, in much simplified form, of one approach to conceptualizing family health, the Circumplex Model. It postulates that healthy families achieve a balance between the extremes of family cohesion, family adaptability, and family communication. Obviously, each healthy family will not be exactly between each extreme (wherever that would be). Some will lean more toward one end or the other, without going too far. This gives rise to a unique mixture of different types of strong families with which we are all acquainted.

Portrait of Strong, Healthy Families

However, readers are still likely to feel somewhat frustrated by this discussion because such a theoretical framework does not give a sufficiently clear picture of what a healthy family is like in the nitty-gritty arena of daily life. The next section of this chapter addresses itself to this issue.

CHARACTERISTICS OF STRONG, HEALTHY FAMILIES

In the process of doing the background work for this chapter, we examined the research of more than a dozen authors who have addressed themselves to the subject of describing and defining healthy, strong, functional families. (Or whatever their choice of term happened to be.) We found ourselves buried under a maze of terms and concepts. Then we began to look for commonalities in the descriptions and found what seemed to us to be a surprising agreement. Having examined the literature, we present the following eight qualities as seeming to us to appear most often among these authors as being characteristic of healthy, strong, functional families. We are aware that several of them overlap, yet we think they are sufficiently different to warrant a separate listing.

1. *Healthy families are good communicators.* We lead off with this because the clearest agreement in all the research on healthy families is that they are effective communicators. This is not surprising. If we think of communication as the ability to transmit a message from the mind of one person to the mind of another, then it is immediately apparent how vital that is to the effective functioning and growth of any relationship. Without clear communication, minor irritations become occasions for major battles, and a loving hug is interpreted as a mauling. The ability to communicate clearly is the basic tool with which family members make decisions and hammer out differences. It is through com-

munication that we let family members know we are dissatisfied with something in the relationship, and it is through communication that we attempt to resolve the issue. But most especially, it is through communication that family members affirm each other through expressions of love and care.

All of this is not to say that healthy families always have nice, calm discussions of issues. The research clearly indicates they sometimes quarrel. But, as we will note later, quarreling is also a way of communicating—of transmitting an idea from one mind to another. But having gotten the issue out in the open, healthy families are able to come to some solution.

An important dimension sometimes overlooked in considering communication is that of listening. Listening is every bit as important in the act of communication as is speaking. In strong, healthy families, members report that they feel listened to. In the act of listening to one another, strong families communicate to others a sense of respect and care. That is, it is a way of saying, "I respect and care enough for you to listen to you."

2. *Healthy families are open in expressing feelings.* It appears that in the strongest and most-functional families, it is possible and safe to be emotionally honest and give expression to feelings—all kinds of feelings, both positive and negative. Of course, this is related to being a good communicator. In less-functional families, the open, honest expression of feelings is discouraged. Rather, family members are taught to be emotional hypocrites. If you are hurt, then smile; if angry, swallow big. It can be dangerous to those who violate the rule. A child who expresses anger to parents in some families meets the threat of getting "teeth knocked down your throat!"

Anger expressed between husband and wife in these

families may also be dangerous. Beyond this, expressions of fear or of inadequacy may bring ridicule or have it thrown up later. It may not even be safe for the husband or wife to express joy or love for fear of being accused of being silly, mushy, manipulative, or otherwise rejected. Thus, in some dysfunctional families, members sit on most of their feelings. In other dysfunctional families, anger builds up and periodically erupts in destructive ways. Family therapists regularly confront this stored-up anger in families with whom they work. So we spend time attempting to get these families to deal with hurt, irritation, anger now rather than doing what George Bach calls "gunny sacking" or storing it up until an explosion takes place.[8]

This open communication of feeling is somewhat analogous to the gauges on your car. Gauges are connected to strategic stress points on the car and keep the driver informed about how these various components are functioning—water temperature, oil pressure, fuel level, alternator. Suppose the oil pressure is dangerously low, but the gauge decides it doesn't want to bother the driver, or fears the driver will get angry if informed. So it keeps silent rather than sounding the alarm. Serious trouble occurs soon. Our feelings are much like those gauges on the car. Thus, the message of anger, or joy, or defeat informs the rest of the family system what is transpiring and corrective measures can be taken if indicated. However, in dysfunctional families, the gauges fail to function properly, so the whole family system suffers. In healthy families, when too much "heat" builds up in one part of the system, corrective measures are taken to relieve the stress; thus the continued smooth functioning of the family system is maintained and assured.

In healthy families, it is not necessary to be emotional hypocrites because:

If angry, you can roar;
   If happy, you can dance;
      If sad, you can weep;
         If filled with excitement, you can jig;
Even if it does look silly for a grown adult to do that!

3. *Healthy families are effective conflict and crisis managers.* Of course, effective conflict and crisis management is unthinkable apart from effective communication. Nonetheless, most authors list this separately and it is important enough, we think, to receive special attention.

It is impossible for people to live together in families without conflicts arising—unless one person is doing all the thinking! Some people are of the opinion that strong families are characterized by an absence of anger, quarreling, or disagreement. Not so! Disagreements do occur in strong families, and on occasion members get angry and perhaps quarrel. Great! You see, as we noted earlier, quarreling is one way people communicate! It may not be the best way, and it certainly isn't the only way, but it is one thoroughly familiar to most of us. It is one way a message is transmitted to another saying, "Something in our relationship is out of balance!" However, quarreling in healthy families is characterized by: *(a)* fighting clean (no name-calling, no physical or personal attacks); *(b)* sticking with the topic; *(c)* being willing to compromise; *(d)* not rejecting the other person. Even in anger there is no question about basic commitment and love for each other; i.e., they do not carry grudges, since having gotten the anger out, the anger soon passes and they go on as before.

Having said this about quarreling, let us emphasize that while most healthy families quarrel on occasion, quarreling is not *necessary* to effective family functioning. There are those families who for a variety of reasons find it intensively distressing to quarrel. For these, quarreling may not be necessary or wise. What *is* vital is that the issue at hand be faced and resolved.

Healthy families also seem able to cope effectively with family crises. Some people mistakenly think that the main difference between strong and troubled families is that the strong ones have few or no crises. Wrong again! Strong families also confront the crises of illness, death, accidents, job changes, moves, as do other families. (To be sure, troubled families often create additional crises by muddling the crisis at hand.) The major difference between healthy and unhealthy families is: *Healthy families know how to get themselves out of their crisis!* In time of crisis, strong families feel they can rely on each other for support. In dysfunctional families, a person may feel very much alone. Rather than feeling that their bonds have been strengthened, dysfunctional families often feel fragmented by the crisis.

4. *Healthy families have structure without rigidity.* This point is related to the Circumplex Model regarding adaptability. Olson, Russell, and Sprenkle define adaptability as "the ability of a marital or family system to change its power structure, role relationships, and relationship rules in response to situational and developmental stress."[9] In other words, a healthy family has rules that govern the ways in which members relate to each other and thereby meet the individual and corporate needs; each family member has a role or roles to carry out in the family which helps avoid chaos and unpredictability in the family. But none of these rules or roles is etched immutably in granite. All can be renegotiated as circumstances change. But in the meanwhile, the family does have structure which gives it a sense of predictability, direction, and security.

"Developmental stress" is mentioned in the above definition. An example of this is the kind of stress created for the wife by the children growing up and leaving home. A change will most certainly be indicated in the roles, rules, and power structure of that family. Or developmental stress expresses itself in the need of a child for more freedom of choice as he or she grows older. Alert parents know how to make adjustments at these times.

Strong, healthy families avoid the extreme of having too much family structure and thereby becoming too rule-bound; but they also avoid having too little structure and thereby becoming chaotic with few values and rules to serve as guidelines for the family. On the other hand, when the rules, roles, values, and power structure of the healthy family cease to meet family needs, they can change.

5. *Healthy families have a strong sense of family bonding, loyalty, and identity.* Members of these families seem to have a clear sense of belonging, of a sense of "familyness." By contrast, members of dysfunctional families have little sense of belonging, of being "rooted" in a family (unless they are enmeshed, in which case the bonds squeeze the individuality out of a person). Children from strong families have a clear family identity as a Sharp or a Keeton. To use Paul Tournier's concept in *A Place for You*, these children have a "place." Nick Stinnett notes that the strong families in his research express this sense of relatedness by making it a point of spending time together. When outside activities begin to make too many inroads on family time, they prune back those outside activities.[10]

In healthy families the members have a strong sense of loyalty to each other. This is another way of saying that they are committed to each other. A member need not feel defensive or protective or cautious in sharing deeply with the family, because a comforting inner sense of security exists which reassures the person that he or she is "in good hands." The person feels that the family has his or her best interests at heart. Not so with less-functional families. In these families it is not safe to be open or to share deeply, for one runs the risk of having the confidence betrayed, or the information used against one, or in some other way being put on the defensive. In these families, the rule is to play it safe and keep one's mouth shut.

One of the more misunderstood terms related to the family is "togetherness." In the '50s and '60s this became a code word for successful family living. Some seemed to think that if a little togetherness made for a good marriage, then a lot of togetherness created a kind of supermarriage! So some supermarriage aspirants tried to do everything together—eat, sleep, play, work, worship, fish, and golf! They were the Ideal American Family. This much togetherness became something like Junior's spinach—it tastes awful, but it is supposed to be good for you! As noted earlier in this chapter, family therapists now recognize that too much cohesion (togetherness) is not healthy, since it thwarts the development of one's own sense of identity and autonomy. In healthy families, there is a balance between too much togetherness and too little.

6. *Healthy families respect the child's uniqueness and individuality.* Though members of families that are strong and healthy have a sense of bonding and committedness to each other, this is balanced by recognition that each adult, each child is a separate person in his or her own right. Juanita remembers someone saying to her, "But your two children are so different!" To this she replied: "What a nice compliment. Perhaps that means our family has permitted them to develop as unique individuals."

A danger we parents confront, and one often stumbled into by less-functional families, is that we have so much emotional investment in our children that we fail to give them freedom to develop in ways that are consistent with their own personalities. Therefore, we exert undue pressure on them to live up to *our* dream for them rather than helping them to dream their own dream; we expect them to dance to our music rather than helping them to make their own music; we want them to accept our values uncritically, rather than helping them to embrace their own values; we want them to drink from the spring of our life rather than helping them to discover their own spring. Most of us are egocentric enough that we are flattered to discover that our child is like us. Healthy parents seem to know how to embrace the child tightly in infancy and then spend the rest of the time gradually letting go, so that this flower can blossom in its own unique way. This should not be interpreted to mean that parents have no expectations of the child, for the child seems to need these.

In the healthiest families, parents seem to communicate to the child:

If you are outgoing or retiring,
that's all right, since we don't all have to be extroverted in our family;
If you are musically inclined or nonmusically inclined,
that's all right, since we don't all have to be musicians in our family;
If you are athletically inclined or nonathletically inclined,
that's all right, since we don't all have to be athletes in our family;
If you are mechanically inclined or nonmechanically inclined,
that's all right, since we don't all have to be handy with hands in our family.
Because in our family I am free to be me, and you are free to be you!

7. *In healthy families, the husband-wife bond is strong, giving them clear leadership in the family.* A clear thread woven

Portrait of Strong, Healthy Families

throughout the literature on healthy families is a theme that in these families there is a strong bond between husband and wife, giving them, not the children, leadership of the family. That is, there is a "coalition," to use a term which this literature often uses, between the mother and the father. This husband-wife bond is stronger than the parent-child bond and certainly stronger than any other loyalties outside the family—friends, in-laws, or one's parents. This is not a matter of "who loves whom the most" but rather a clear model for the children that a special relationship exists between the parents, one that transcends the parent-child relationship, and will continue even after the children are grown and gone. Because of this special relationship, the parents are strong enough to provide security for the children and provide the nurture and love they need. In disturbed families, that parental bond is weak and children are often able to exploit it by a "divide and conquer" maneuver. The parents end up quarreling with each other and feeling alienated, while the children go do what they wanted to do anyway.

Having said this about parental leadership, we have some concern that this may be interpreted to mean that parents exercise a heavy-handed authoritarian, "do it because I say so" leadership. Not so! We have already indicated that parents in healthy families value and respect the integrity and uniqueness of each child. Parental leadership and authority, like leadership and authority in general, is best worn lightly, but with a clear awareness that it is there. There should be no question in the minds of the children as to who is in charge of the family. Yet they know that they can have input into family decisions and know that as they grow older and more responsible, the parents will delegate to them increasing decision-making powers about their own lives. It is because the parents are strong and support each other that they are able to offer security and protection to the children. The child who views the parents as weak and manipulatable is unable to feel secure, since *only strength can protect*. To be sure, each child will "test the limits" and fuss and complain about parental restrictions, but while one part of the child hopes the maneuver will cause the parent to capitulate and give in, another part wants the parent to stand fast and thereby reassure him or her that the parent is strong.

8. *In healthy families the members do much affirming of each other.* To affirm another means that in a variety of ways we do and say things which communicate to the other person that we value him or her. Disturbed families are usually characterized by much picking, criticizing, nagging, and put-downs. In various and sundry ways they in effect say to the other person, "You are inadequate"; "There is something wrong with you"; "I don't value you." On the other hand, strong families in a host of ways communicate to others that they are viewed as adequate, competent, and worthwhile.

Myron Madden's book *The Power to Bless* has as its central thesis the idea that each person has it in his or her power to bless (affirm) another person.[11] You bless others as you help them to feel good about themselves. But it is also true that, in effect, each person has the power to pronounce a "curse" upon another by disaffirming the other. Too much of, "Are you dumb or something?" or "Can't you ever do anything right?" can curse a child by planting doubts in his or her mind about being competent, worthwhile, valued. On the other hand, "Great job!" and "I love you!" pronounce a blessing.

William James, noted psychologist at the turn of the century, said, "The deepest longing in the human breast is the desire for appreciation." We might argue whether it is the deepest desire, but it is unquestionably one of the deep desires we all possess. One of the ways family members affirm one another is by expressing appreciation. Few of us have to look far to find something for which we can genuinely express appreciation to someone close to us. You can think of other ways to affirm one another.

One day while walking across the parking lot of a local shopping center, one of us (Wallace) spotted a piece of paper blowing across the lot with something written on it. Ah, a secret! Chasing it down, I discovered these words written in a child's scrawl on that scrap of paper, "I love Dad and I love Mom and THEY LOVE ME!" I don't know who that child is, but I know that somewhere in our town is a blessed child. I know that the child is blessed or it could not be giving back this love to the parents and thereby affirm them. That child has been loved well by the parents, because you cannot give that which you have not received.

Thus, we come to the end of this discussion of strong, healthy families. As stated at the beginning of the chapter, we view what has been said here as foundational to much of what will follow. Much of it will be said again, in different ways, throughout the book. Though the healthy families we have discussed have much in common with each other, we would conclude the chapter by reminding you of two things:

First, despite their commonalities, there is still much latitude for differentness between strong families. That is, all strong families are not alike. Some have more structure than others, some have more cohesion than others, some will be better communicators than others. Yet, all of them operate within the broad limits of being sufficiently competent in vital areas for the family to function quite successfully. *There is no one pattern for successful family living.* This is the major criticism we have of books purporting to tell us what Christian families are like. They would usually have us believe there is only *one* pattern for *the* Christian family. As a matter of fact, there are many different types of healthy families (including healthy Christian families), because each family brings together the basic ingredients of a strong family in its own unique ways, much as different cooks take the same ingredients and turn out quite different tasting products because of the unique mix of ingredients provided by each cook.

Secondly, no one family achieves all the ingredients of healthy family living at the optimal level. Each family to a greater or lesser degree is both successful and unsuccessful in each area. It may be that in some area the family is rather deficient, yet in other areas is so competent that the total family system continues to function quite effectively.

Having examined what the current research suggests to us as being qualities of the strongest and healthiest families, we trust this exploration has stimulated you to an examination of your own family. We hope it has affirmed you in some areas, and provoked you to resolve to work on other areas of your strong family. Remember: You don't have to have a sick family to make it better!

3
Enriching Your Sexual Relationship

SEX! Those three letters invariably ring bells in the minds of all men and women. For some it is the ringside bell signaling time for another round in their marital battle. For others it is the cash register bell, for sex sells autos, deodorants, shoes, and other heart's desires. For yet others, it is the fire bell, since the word ignites the flames of desire. But it is the burglar alarm for some, signaling an unwanted intrusion into their lives. The word makes them uptight. One cannot be neutral about sex. The very word evokes some emotion in every person.

Sexual desire has given rise to some of our loftiest literature and liveliest songs. It has inspired noble deeds and grisly murders. It has led kings to flaunt the conventions of society and abandon their wives, and the common man to consort with harlots. It has motivated great generosity, and inspired heroic self-sacrifice. Sex has made the sick healthy, and the healthy sick. It has made the wealthy poor, and the poor wealthy. Sex is so central to our lives that from the cradle to the grave, we cannot ignore its impact. In fact, the first question asked about most of us was sexual, "Boy or girl?" The answer to the question immediately determined the type of name we got, and the color of the blanket in which we were wrapped.

So central is sex to our lives that Willard Waller and Reuben Hill assert:

> The sexual impulse can be conditioned to different forms of expression, modified to fit the social order, harnessed to do the work of the world, curbed and encouraged and frustrated and hammered out of shape. But it can never be completely eliminated, never wholly denied, nor can its essential character be destroyed.[12]

Though sex is the source of some of our greatest pleasure, satisfaction, and fulfillment, let us be honest and admit that it is also the source of some of our greatest frustration, anxiety, and pain. It may be that the only way to live with sex with any degree of comfort is to take it seriously, but not *too* seriously. Sex, like the rest of life, is much too serious not to be taken with a measure of humor! Tom Driver believes that the ability to laugh at sex is essential if one is to live comfortably with this powerful force. He says:

> Laughter at sex is about the only way to put sex in its place, to assert one's humanity over against that impersonal, irrational, yet necessary force that turns even the best of men into caricatures of themselves. Not only "sinful" sex does this: lawful sex, safely within the limits of marriage and love does it too, as everybody knows; and he who does not laugh about it must be humiliated by it.[13]

This chapter is written for those fellow travelers who, like ourselves, are attempting to maximize the meaningfulness of this dimension of life, and minimize the frustration and pain. From the laughter, tears, and smiles of those with whom we have worked in therapy (not to mention our own experience), we have learned a few things about enriching this part of life. One thing we have learned is that it is an ongoing process. That is, a meaningful sexual relationship is a dynamic rather than static process. One never has it "in the bag" for long. Life changes too much for that kind of durability.

We are not among those who believe that good marriages begin and end in the bedroom. We know couples who have warm and loving relationships, but whose sex lives are deficient by most standards. Then we have talked with other couples who are ready for a divorce and who have trouble getting along anywhere together, except in bed. Strange! To understand this, we must recognize that the total relationship and individual personalities must be taken into account. (This is not to say that the couple with a poor sexual relationship like it that way; rather, that poor sex does not *necessarily* threaten the continuation of the marriage—if they have a rewarding relationship in other areas and do not view a satisfying sex life as imperative to the relationship.) However, for most of us, at least a reasonably satisfying sexual relationship is considered necessary to a good marital relationship.

O. Spurgeon English and Gerald H. Pearson likely speak for many of us when they assert, "When sexual adjustment in marriage is good, it constitutes about ten percent of the positive part, but when sexual adjustment is bad, it constitutes about ninety percent of what is wrong.[14] One of the first places a poor marital relationship usually manifests itself is in the bedroom. At the same time, we do not believe that sexual difficulties are always symptomatic of a poor relationship in other areas. Sometimes the sexual difficulty *is* the problem, not the symptom.

Sex and Western Culture

Despite the current openness about sex, many of us from all age groups have grown up in environments in which sex is as hush-hush and forbidden as ever. Juanita still remembers when after marriage she discovered the wonderful freedom that sex can be talked about comfortably as a normal, and important, part of life. Wallace grew up on a farm where you would think the sex lives of the animals would have been a kind of sex education, but he remembers being told that the cow "found" a calf. When cattle were breeding, all small children (and females of any age) were hurriedly rushed into the house lest they view the unviewable! A high school vocational agriculture teacher referred to a bull as a "gentleman cow." So farm life did not help many of us as children. In any case, younger children often fail to make the transition of thought between animals and people.

Though sex is usually a respectable topic for discussion in churches today, not too long ago it was never mentioned from the pulpit except in heavy condemnatory terms of adulterous behavior. Though he remembers no one teaching him this, as an adolescent Wallace believed that the fall of man in the Garden of Eden had something to do with sex. Later, he discovered that other churchgoers believed the same thing. Erroneously we reached the conclusion that the sin of Adam and Eve was sex. After all, what other kind of temptation is there? (Few realize that many centuries earlier, St. Augustine also concluded that Adam and Eve's sin was sex.)

In his classic book, *Sex in Christianity and Psychoanalysis*, William Graham Cole traces the history of the fear, suspicion, and discomfort with sex in Western thought.[15] In brief, Cole traces this discomfort back to ancient Middle Eastern dualistic thinking, particularly Zoroastrianism, which divided man into body and spirit. Dualists generally viewed the body as evil, along with all appetites of the body, especially sex. Through the conquests of Alexander the Great, his soldiers became introduced to this dualistic thinking and brought it back to Greece, where it infiltrated Hellenistic thinking. Man was divided into body and spirit and came to be viewed as *having* a soul. The ancient Hebrews did not say that man *has* a soul but *is* a soul which includes the body and all that we are (Gen. 2:7). By New Testament times, there were numerous dualistic groups contending for the loyalties of the people. One of these, the Gnostics, attempted to infiltrate early Christian thought with their negative views of sex and the body. The Gospel of John specifically attempts to counter this influence by affirming the goodness of the body in asserting that "the Word became flesh" (John 1:14). Horror of horrors to devout Gnostics! They taught that Jesus only *appeared* to have a body.

The ancient Hebrews, Cole says, had a naturalistic understanding of sex. This understanding, however, was lost by the early church fathers, who, like all educated people of the day, were well-grounded in Hellenistic Greek thinking. As a result of this influence, they sometimes unwittingly "baptized" into Christian theology dualistic ideas which were pagan in origin. (A fuller treatment of this subject is found in Chapters 1 and 2 of Cole's book.)

About a century ago a movement was launched to liberate sex from the bondage in which it had been held so long. Havelock Ellis, Sigmund Freud, and the late Alfred Kinsey were pioneers in this effort to free sex from the constraints of the unconscious, and shadows of ignorance and repression. Now that sex is "out of the closet," and considered respectable company for "nice people," the Western world seems bent on making up for lost time. Sex has been "evangelistically" filmed, taped, printed, photographed, recorded, advertised, and researched. But society may have traded the old *repression* for a new form of *oppression*—a demand for performance. Whereas men and women once were pressured to repress sexual urges, an active sexual life has become almost mandatory for contemporary men and women—unless one wants to be viewed as inhibited, strange, or incomplete. Instead of feeling guilty over having sex, many modern Americans feel guilty over not being sexually active! The twenty-two-year-old man who sought help because he was still a virgin and felt "out of it" exemplifies this group. But this oppression is not confined to the unmarried, for married couples eagerly consult researchers to determine whether they are keeping up with the "average American." Shame on the couple who is below average!

Schools of Sexual Enrichment

It is sometimes said that Americans are doing it more and enjoying it less than previous generations. At least there is some support for the thesis that we are doing it more. The best evidence is that today's couple has intercourse more frequently than grandma and grandpa did. Yet the popularity of sex manuals proposing to help that couple's sex life suggests that the couple want more of something out of all this sexual activity. We have observed five schools of thought holding forth the "holy grail" of better sex to frustrated modern couples.

1. *The Mother Nature School* teaches that all the talk, books, films, and television about sex are to blame for the modern couple's frustration. The media have polluted the

Enriching Your Sexual Relationship 57

couple's minds. "Leave them alone," this school teaches, "and what Mother Nature and experience don't teach them, they don't need to know anyway." Some people in this group are opposed to sex education, especially in the schools. (Some give lip service to sex education at home, but their children whom we have taught appear to be as sexually illiterate as the next child.)

2. *The Cookbook School* is founded on the premise that a good sexual relationship can be achieved by following the recipe. So advocates of this school read, read. Good sex is a matter of correct information and proper technique. Those with sexual problems just haven't learned the right buttons to press. This is "sex by the numbers." Thus, a man is instructed to first kiss her here, then stroke there, finally fondle that. By this time he has a tiger on his hands! It is easy if you follow the recipe. Some of you may remember those sex manuals which spotted all the "erogenous zones" on the body. Eager high school and college fellows memorized these places hoping to kiss, rub, and stroke their dates into a passionate frenzy! (Of course, we now know that the whole body is an erogenous zone.)

To be sure, the Cookbook School has an important point to make in its valuation of the importance of knowledge about sexual functioning. No thinking person can depreciate that. However, though knowledge and technique are important, it is naive to believe that the mere spreading of knowledge and development of smooth techniques are the secret "open sesame" to a rewarding sex life. Knowledge and technique are *necessary* but not *sufficient*. The quality of the relationship between the couple is also vital. As Howard Gadlin warns, "Technical training by itself, severed from social relations, directs people toward performance, not fulfillment."[16]

3. *The Driver Education School* teaches that the road to

sexual richness requires some "time behind the wheel." Some exponents of this point of view even say that one needs wide-ranging experience with several autos since there are so many different types—manual shifts, automatic transmissions, front-wheel drives, rear-wheel drives, big cars, little cars—and each requires a different set of skills to master.

The problem with this school, it seems to us, is that we have seen numerous couples in therapy over the years who were widely experienced sexually prior to marriage with no apparent difficulty, but who have sexual difficulties now that they are married. We have known other couples who lived together prior to marriage without sexual difficulties but who have developed such problems soon after saying "I do." Just as there is now research suggesting that driver education in the schools does not produce better drivers, we have yet to be convinced that either wide sexual experience with many partners prior to marriage or an extensive sexual relationship with the future mate contributes to a higher level of marital sexual satisfaction than couples without this experience.

Fleeting sexual relationships with numerous persons or sex with a "live in" partner are not adequate measures of future marital sexual fulfillment. In fact, Kinsey found that persons who were widely experienced prior to marriage were also more likely to become involved in extramarital sexual relationships than their inexperienced colleagues.[17] Extramarital relationships usually have a devastating impact on the marriage.

4. *The More-Is-Better School* is sure that if a little does a little good, then a whole lot should do a whole lot of good. Thus, members of this group are preoccupied with norms, averages, and means. How much, how often, how big, the "average" is of preeminent concern. If they find that the

typical couple in their age bracket has intercourse three times a week, they will try for at least 3.5 times! (That .5 may be frustrating!) Thus, the sexual relationship degenerates into a field of competition in which the couple attempt to keep up with or outdo what "they" are doing rather than celebrate their own relationship in their own way.

5. *The Exotica School* is sure that the path to better sex lies in developing, discovering, and conjuring up some new and exotic sexual practice. Its exponents view with disdain whatever the typical couple might do as being uncreative, unimaginative, and mundane. None of that for them! They seek that which is new, different, exotic. Thus, they eagerly search ancient sex manuals from India, China, or Greece hoping to find that which is novel. Like the Athenians of old, they worship at the shrine of the new and novel (Acts 17:21). They become preoccupied with unusual positions, places, music, incense, costumes, vibrators, dildos, leather, and chains. Their bedrooms look like the annex to a hardware store! One husband of our acquaintance would go to considerable expense and spend days constructing elaborate leather and chain harnesses for his wife to wear while he filmed her trying to escape from the outfit. Yet none of this was really satisfying to him for long, and he was often impotent. She complained of feeling like nothing more than a prop for his movies. She was ready to make love, not perform on camera! (Of course, she did go along with all of this.)

We do not think there is *necessarily* anything wrong with any of the above, if a couple *mutually find them to be meaningful*. To be sure, our sexual lives often fall into a routine that may leave one or both partners wishing for something new. (We will say more on this later.) Rather, what we are concerned with here is the obsessive-compulsive pursuit of novelty and the ignoring of a relationship. (In any case, some of the exotic positions described in the manuals require a gymnast to get into them, and once there, you can't do anything!)

Having explored these schools of thought to a more rewarding sexual relationship, none of which we particularly recommend, let us turn to some positive steps that we think couples can take to enrich this dimension of life.

Toward Enriching Your Sexual Relationship

Since the term "enrich" suggests adding richness to something that already has a measure of richness, this part of the chapter (and indeed the whole book) is addressed to couples who consider themselves to have a basically satisfactory sexual relationship, but who want to enhance that relationship. The suggestions to follow will likely do no good for couples with serious sexual difficulties. On the other hand, one of our assumptions is that every couple, including those who consider themselves to have good relationships, can profitably spend time devoting attention to enriching their sexual lives. Rather than focus on specific techniques, we will devote attention to what we consider to be more fundamental principles of sexual enrichment.

1. *Keeping an open telephone line*, we believe, is basic to any meaningful sexual relationship. This is another way of underlining the primacy of good communication. One of the strange anomalies of our culture is that despite the open depiction of sex by the media, hordes of couples seldom discuss their own sexual lives. People in our society deal with sex indirectly through jokes, films, photographs, novels about sex in *other* people. Much less often is the focus on "you and me." When couples do talk of their own relationship, it is too often done only when pressures have built up in anger and frustration. In this case, a lot of words

are said, but there is likely little communication. A rewarding and liberating experience reported by many couples is the discovery that they can openly and safely discuss their sexual likes and dislikes, joys and frustrations. This is not easy, but it is worth pursuing.

One of the major positive things that we see happening in marriage enrichment groups is that couples start talking openly and frankly about their relationship, often for the first time. Couples are surprised to discover that both are unhappy with an aspect of their relationship. They may open the door for a fantasy to come true. For instance, one husband was delighted to discover that his wife would sometimes like to have sex during the day on the living room carpet, a fantasy he had toyed with but did not dare mention.

Without communication, couples condemn themselves to continuing their mistakes, since they have rejected the basic "tool" for bringing about change.

2. *Broadening your view of a sexual relationship* is needed by many people. Some of us have such a narrow view of sex. Only intercourse is seen as sex. We also need to discover that a kiss is sex, an embrace is sex, touching is sex, a warm and intimate conversation is sex, cuddling in bed is sex, a romantic dinner by candlelight is sex. This point was captured by a middle-aged man attending a seminar we were conducting when he announced to the group that he and his wife had sex every day. The group was momentarily taken aback by such frequency until he continued, "Of course, we have intercourse much less often." He went on to explain that he had discovered that a wide variety of experiences were sexual other than just intercourse.

Men, in particular, suffer from "sexual myopia." Sex to them is too often confined to a penis in a vagina. That is sex all right, but that view cheats a man out of so much other possible sexual delight. Thus, a common complaint heard from wives is, "I'm afraid to hug him because he starts angling me toward the bedroom." "Sometimes," they say, "I'd like to just cuddle and be close without it always having to end in intercourse." This idea is alien to hordes of men who have a narrow view of sex. Is it conditioning? Probably. In any case, a broadening of one's understanding of sex would enrich the relationships.

3. *Becoming more comfortable inside your head* will enrich the sexual relationship. As has often been noted, the head is the greatest sex organ. No one can function sexually more satisfyingly than his or her head—i.e., attitudes, knowledge, values—will permit. Even if you consider yourself to have a good sexual relationship, you likely have some vestigial old attitudes, values, taboos from your childhood which in some measure short-circuit your sexual life. These self-defeating elements have to do with feelings about yourself (self-esteem), attitudes about the opposite sex, or attitudes about sex in general. For instance, a boy growing up in an environment where women are viewed primarily as housekeepers and attractive playmates for men will likely have difficulty relating to his wife when she insists on being respected as a competent, intelligent copartner in the marriage. A wife whose mother taught her as a girl that "sex is a trick that nature plays on us to perpetuate the race" has a mental handicap that was sure to make it difficult for her to maximize the meaningfulness of sex in her life.

The head also short-circuits the sexual relationship in yet another way—through mental stagnation and boredom. People who are bored with life, with themselves, with each other, and who have stagnated in their thinking, are not likely to make good sex partners for long. The bored need to break out of the numbing routine of their lives. Others suffer from mental stagnation because they have not

Enriching Your Sexual Relationship

thought any new thoughts, or read any new books for a long, long time. These need to read, attend a seminar, take a class, do anything to liven up the stagnant pool of the mind. (We are not talking of books and classes on sex.)

Outdated and self-defeating attitudes and values, mental stagnation, and boredom are all processes of the head that spoil good sex. You can write it down: If you are dead in the head, you are dead in bed!

4. *Becoming more comfortable inside your own skin* will enrich a sexual relationship. Since sex involves all that we are, we cannot develop a good sexual relationship unless we become comfortable both within our heads and within our own skins—i.e., with our physical selves. (To be sure, these two are intimately related; we separate them here for emphasis.) Those who are not comfortable with their physical selves are not good candidates for a rich sexual life.

As we listen to husbands and wives talk uncomfortably of their physical selves, at times it seems as if we hear the ghosts of old dualists who many centuries ago declared the body to be evil. These ghosts manifest themselves in those who sit so uncomfortably inside their skins. Bodily urges make them ill at ease. Others have a "poor body image" and see themselves as ugly, fat, skinny, poorly proportioned. (The fact that others might see them as attractive is no consolation.) Also, we are amazed by how many women have never looked at their genitals. They have often spent a lifetime looking and touching themselves as little as possible. No wonder such women are uptight about sex!

Not only are couples often uncomfortable and unacquainted with their own bodies, they are ignorant of and uncomfortable with the mate's body. Though married for years, they may have caught only fleeting glimpses of each other in the nude. In this case, we instruct them to several times look, touch, examine each other's genitals and ask questions about which parts are most sensitive. These exercises sometimes provoke great anxiety in one or both partners (the best evidence of the need for the exercise). They may view this as strange or perverted, but the purpose is to desensitize the discomfort one has about his or her own body or the mate's body, and begin to develop an appreciation for the beauty and marvelous wonders of this gift from God—the body. If sex means anything, it is not only a celebration of a relationship, but it is also a celebration of our physical selves. You cannot celebrate the physical if you are not comfortable inside your own skin.

5. *Following your own drumbeat* will enrich your sexual life. By this we encourage you to pursue that kind of relationship and experience which is *mutually meaningful* to the two of you. Why worry about what the average couple does? Do your own thing! If you mutually enjoy sex four or forty times a month, who cares what the average couple does?

We would also like to see our society get away from terms such as "abnormal" and "perverted" as they are typically used regarding sex. We want to go beyond what people usually think of when "perverted" is used. We believe people pervert sex by using it as a means of expressing anger. Thus, sex becomes a way for punishing the mate through withholding it or perhaps engaging in unusual roughness. Others pervert sex by using it as a way of manipulating the mate. For example, the wife who will relate sexually to the husband only when he has "behaved himself" and done the laundry or bought her something is being manipulative. We believe that sex either as manipulation or as a way of punishment is perversion. It seems to us that no practice that *you both find mutually satisfying* in the privacy of your bedroom should be called perverted or abnormal. People differ widely in their sexual preferences,

Enriching Your Sexual Relationship

as they do in other arenas of life. We believe that having informed themselves about the subject, a couple need to talk with each other and work out for themselves what they personally find meaningful. Whether others do, or do not do, the same thing is irrelevant. Do your own thing!

However, you will note we have used the term "mutual" several times. If one does not enjoy or find meaningful a particular experience, then we think the other partner ought not insist on it. Nonetheless, we often do not like something simply because we have not tried it. So experiment! You may also need to experiment long enough to get over the shock of its newness.

6. *Adding variety to the sexual relationship* will enrich most marriages. A major threat to a sexually satisfying relationship is routine, monotony, and the resultant boredom. (However, in keeping with the point just made, if you like routine, don't dare change!) "Same time, same station" often becomes the motto of our sexual lives. We do everything, every time, in exactly the same way, same time, same place. Nothing is new! No surprises! The usual result: no excitement, no satisfaction.

The price paid for monotony and routine is the loss of sensitivity, the loss of celebration, and sometimes the development of erratic behavior. Most people suffer in silence. The person may not even be aware of what we call the "dry rot."[18] But the hidden malaise may express itself in a frantic search for fun and pleasure, or in anger, lethargy, moodiness, or the difficulty in focusing on work or family. For some, more and more erotic movies, sex magazines, and topless bars may have to be added to the bored person's routine to keep the sexual fires lighted in a dead relationship.

If variety is the spice of life, what can be done? Do something different! As noted earlier in the chapter, we do not think it is necessary to worship at the shrine of the novel in order to break out of the stifling prison of routine. We remember a couple who injected new life into their stagnated sexual life by simply doffing the night clothes and sleeping nude. Sexual fantasies can often point the way to new life. For instance, one husband was surprised (and thrilled) to discover his wife sometimes had fantasies of him slowly and quietly completely undressing her and taking her to bed. (If these suggestions make you uncomfortable, you may need to go back to the point of "becoming comfortable in your own head.")

7. *Developing a more caring and loving relationship* will enrich your sexual life. John Levy and Ruth Monroe are exactly on target when they assert that "the quality of love depends on the lovers."[19] Lovers who are not loving will likely not have a very satisfying sex life. Technique is important, but the emotional side of sex is equally important. Most sex research to date has focused on people's ability to perform and has largely ignored the emotional side of sex. As a result, sex therapist Raul Schiavi says, "We're becoming aware that people who are perfectly capable of having orgasms and erections can have problems because they don't feel like performing."[20] Without a rich emotional relationship, sex becomes unfulfilling. Without a sense of loving care, intercourse leaves one feeling empty. Each person has done something *to* the other, but not *with* the other.

Unless you are married to a selfish, insensitive egoist, an investment in being a more caring, giving, and loving person will pay real dividends by enriching the whole marriage, and specifically the sexual relationship.

In conclusion, you have noted that throughout this chapter, we have repeatedly used the term "sexual relation ship." This reflects our belief that though sex is a physical response, to be enduringly rewarding it must also be a *relationship*. Sex divorced from a relationship ultimately becomes an empty experience for both partners. Without a relationship, sex is nothing more than copulation, a joining of genitals. We believe that the most enduringly satisfying sexual relationship takes place when:

>Two whole persons,
>>Committed to each other in loving care,
>>>Freely and uninhibitedly,
>
>Celebrate their relationship through sex.

4
Guidelines for Living with Children

Rearing children has all the drama, suspense, adventure, and intrigue of a best-selling novel. A major difference is that if the novel gets too tense, you can turn to the last chapter to see how things turn out. Oh, that parenthood were that way! Anxiety over how the "story" will turn out is a major frustration of parenthood. If we could just be assured that our children will turn out all right, then we could relax and enjoy it more. Unfortunately, with parenthood each chapter has to be lived in sequence, with no real guarantee as to what the final chapter will contain.

What do concerned parents do to cope with their anxiety while waiting for their children to grow up? Tens of thousands turn to books written by experts—and have thereby made a few of these authors wealthy! Some experts speak with much more dogmatism than their knowledge and experience merit. Others suggest in the opening pages that parents should not pay too much attention to experts (they should trust themselves!) and then proceed, chapter after chapter, to give advice on every facet of parenting. Some are parents themselves, though one of the better-known authors had no children of his own, his experiences with children being largely confined to nieces and nephews.

We submit that occasional contacts with nieces and nephews is a universe away from living with your own children day after day, year after year!

We would not want to add unnecessarily to the confusion of modern parents by joining other family specialists and parading out a catalog of rules for child-rearing. (We are convinced that anyone who professes to know much about how to rear *your* children will lie about other things, too!) Nonetheless, our twenty-five years of experience in working with troubled families, conducting dozens of family enrichment conferences, reading the literature, teaching family relationships, and rearing our two children (now grown) have taught us a few things about parenting. We share them with you for your consideration. You can determine whether they are relevant to your role as a parent.

If there is anything we have learned, it is that modern parents do not need to feel any more anxious and guilty than they already do. Max Lerner has observed that perhaps no parents anywhere are more anxious about being good parents than American parents.[21] The "there is only one way to rear children" approach, in addition to being wrong, also heaps great amounts of anxiety and guilt on modern parents. As a matter of fact, there are numerous effective ways to rear children, as any careful observer of families is aware. Nonetheless, we believe there are certain basic commonalities that cut across all these approaches.

We want to deal with what we believe are some of the basic issues involved with living with children in the family. For some parents, these issues are emotionally tense ones. Remember the furor created by Ann Landers several years ago when she conducted a poll through her column, asking the question, "Parenthood—if you had a choice, would you do it again?" Of those ten thousand who responded, nearly three quarters said they were sorry they became parents. She concluded, after all the responses were in, that the hurt, angry, and disenchanted tend to write more readily than the contented. Also, she suggested that, just maybe, people told her things they would not dare tell anyone else.

Becoming a parent is much like the "point of no return" on an overseas trip: once a parent, there is no turning back. The longevity of the role adds to the anxiety. As Alice Rossi observes, "We have ex-spouses and ex-jobs, but no ex-children."[22] Parents may divorce each other, but becoming a parent is a lifetime arrangement—"for better for worse, for richer for poorer . . . till death us do part." Furthermore, having grown children in the home (those who never left, or left and came back because of divorce or unemployment) is becoming much more common and making "frontline" parenting longer and longer.

Children and the Marriage Relationship

What does or can all of this concern over the children do to a marriage? Much has been written on the negative impact of parents on children, but it is also true that the arrival of a child may be hazardous to the well-being of the marriage. As family therapists, we often see couples, who, it appears, got along quite well until the child came. Some middle-aged couples report that their marriage improved significantly after the children left home. Living with children definitely influences the relationship of the parents.

The quality of the marital relationship may decline after the birth of a child because one or both partners invest so much time and emotional energy in the newcomer that they have little left for each other. This is partly understandable, since being a parent demands much time and energy.

However, parents sometimes attempt to derive too many of their emotional needs from the relationship with the child long after the newcomer stage. When parents invest too much energy in the children, both the children and the marriage lose. What do children gain from the attention that parents give each other? For one thing, it removes the burden from children of having to meet needs of the parents that should be coming from the marital relationship. This gives the children greater freedom to develop their own identities and personalities.

To state this problem somewhat differently, Howard and Charlotte Clinebell say that the point at which many marriages "jump the track is overinvesting in the children and underinvesting in the marriage."[23] Out of her years working with children, Dorothy Briggs concludes that when parents attempt to maneuver their children into meeting needs of the marital relationship, the parents end up angry with the children when they fail—as the children inevitably must do. The more satisfying the marriage, she notes, the freer we are to let our child develop his or her personality, since the child is not expected to fill the vacuum left by an empty marriage.[24]

We would emphasize that we are writing about extremes—overinvesting and underinvesting. Neglecting one relationship, spouse or child, does not improve another. All of life's important relationships need an emotional investment. The real task is establishing the proper balance. Taking inventory of the marital relationship is needed on a regular basis, both for the sake of the parents and the child.

We have attempted to establish the fact that the transition from being a childless couple to becoming a parent is one of the major transitions of life. In view of this, it is strange that so little is done to help equip parents for this demanding role. Often something as simple as having groups of parents meet together, and discover that their concerns are very much like others', can be most helpful. We believe that living with children can bring much more joy and satisfaction if we can create a more supportive environment in which to rear them. A more supportive community can help us come to grow as parents, and in turn permits us to provide opportunities for letting our children grow as persons.

PARENT'S SURVIVAL KIT

One way we would like to be more supportive of parents who are eager to do a better job in this significant role is to explore some ideas that might be included in a Parent's Survival Kit. This kit is for parents who have a relatively good relationship with their child. We do not propose to answer all the concerns that parents have (e.g., drugs, teenage sex, runaways) in one chapter. However, if we admit this limitation, what are some of the things that can be done in order to decrease the anxiety of being a parent? Below is our Parent's Survival Kit, which you might keep in mind.

1. *You are not the only influence in the lives of your children.* There are many influences that shape and mold your children. You are an important one, but only one.

The peer group exercises a powerful influence over your children. While parents are the primary agents of influence in the lives of preschoolers, beyond this, peers have a growing impact upon their lives. So great is the peer influence that some authorities say there is practically no value that a young person has which the peer group by concerted effort cannot batter down. The impact of the peer group expresses itself in dress fads, language, musical tastes, and dozens of other ways.

The mass media have a powerful influence on children. We may never understand completely the full impact of television on children (not to mention adults). One estimation is that preschool children spend two thirds of their waking hours in front of the television. In addition, books, records, and magazines leave their impressions to influence the young.

You have no influence over some of these influences. For instance, we are just now beginning to learn some significant things concerning biological influences on children's behavior. That is, genetic factors may influence behavior. This has been especially revealing in some of the university studies concerning identical twins. Even though separated at birth and reared in completely different environments, without knowledge of each other until adulthood, they often display remarkable similarities in behavior and personality.

Any parent with two children is aware of how very different they usually are even though they share the same parents and home. (Of course, no two children ever grow up in identically the same home. The fact that one is older than the other in itself makes a difference.) What we are writing here is that grandma may have been partly right in blaming some of Junior's behavior on "that Henderson blood!" It appears that there may be genetic factors which at least predispose one toward some kinds of behavior.

So, regardless of whether you are evaluating positive or negative behavior in your child, you might remind yourself of this truth: "Since I am not the only influence in my children's lives, I refuse to accept full blame for their problems; I likewise cannot take full credit for all their successes."

2. *You will not be a perfect parent.* Accepting this truth will help you to be a less anxious parent. Attempting to be the

perfect parent is a heavy burden. In any case, what is a perfect parent? No one knows. When we hear a parent say that she promised herself she would never make the same mistakes with her child that her parents made with her, we begin to feel a bit uneasy. We may be seeing the making of a "perfect parent" before us. This concerns us, because "perfect parents" usually try so hard that they often neglect their own personal growth as well as the growth of their marital relationship. They may also become angry with the child, or disgusted with themselves if the child invalidates their "parental perfection" by being less than the perfect child.

Perhaps, at one time, all of us as parents had hoped or planned to be the perfect parent. I (Wallace) once had a lecture on child-rearing and parenthood in which I pontificated mightily. When our first child came, I revised the lecture. When the second child came, I tore it up!

What can a parent do about the need for perfection? Perhaps the best thing is: *Do as well as you reasonably can, and trust God for the rest.* That is usually enough. We also think that parents can save themselves from a lot of unnecessary anxiety if they do not evaluate their competence as parents until the child is at least twenty-five. Until then, they are usually still in the process of "jelling." It is frequently a shock to discover at this time that they are more like us than unlike us. (Assuming that being "like us" is one of our goals.)

3. *Remember, you usually have to consistently do the wrong thing at the right time over a period of years to do real psychological damage to your child.* That is, except in cases of real trauma, a single incident does not usually scar a child for life.

We remember when our son was born. It was a great concern of ours that we do absolutely nothing "to break his spirit." He had not been living with us too many months when we realized that if any spirits were to be broken, they would most likely be ours! Children are much more resilient than we sometimes think.

Doing the wrong thing at times is normal. However, knowing that we have not handled a situation wisely helps us to not repeat the situation. It is important that bad days be redeemed with good ones. If we have made a mistake, we should admit it. It is the quality of these loving, accepting good days that builds the kind of foundation that can handle the stress brought on by the times we think we have done the wrong thing with our child.

4. *Being a good parent does not mean your child will feel warm and loving toward you at all times.* This brings to mind one significant time when we grounded our high school age daughter. Because of this, she was unable to attend what was to her an important social event at school. It was a painful thing for us to do, although she probably would not have believed this at the time. Needless to say, she was angry with us. This did not help our pain. Our strokes came a few years later when she said to me (Juanita) while talking about a friend who was deeply troubled: "What I think Ann's problem is, her parents were never really strict enough with her when she was in high school. She could get away with anything!" This comment from her brought comfort to those past days when Wallace and I felt that warmth and love were a foreign language to her feelings for us as parents.

Good parents sometimes have to make unpopular decisions and their child at that moment will feel much less than warm and loving toward them. However, we believe that it is not necessary that children always have warm feelings toward their parents. We do think it is important for the relationship to merit respect.

5. *As a good parent, you do not always have to put the needs of*

your child first. Some parents appear always to put the needs of their child first. In return they see themselves as martyrs. "Look at all the sacrifices I have made for you," may be the message sent to their child. It may be that being neglected is in some ways easier for a child to handle than being burdened with the guilt of "costing" their parents so much. At least the neglected child sometimes finds parental substitutes in a teacher, a friend's parent, or some other concerned adult. The child of the martyr parent may carry deep scars of guilt around for a lifetime, and never really know how to handle the situation. How can children express anger to a mother or father who sacrified *everything* for them (and often reminded them of this)?

If we examine martyr parents more closely, it will probably become apparent that it is their own needs they are putting first, not those of the child. It may be a need to be praised for their great sacrifices that leads them to put the child in the position of being victim of such "sacrificial love."

Are sacrifices ever needed? We think so! For example, a mother may make a conscious choice to "sacrifice" her career to be at home with a child. She does it, because to her this is the best "professional" use of her time at this stage of life. However, if she begins throwing this up to the child, she has turned a good conscious choice into what sounds like a martyred parent.

6. *Remember: "This too shall pass."* Frequently, when we talk with mothers who are at home with preschool children, we remind them, although they seem to disbelieve us, that their children will not always be preschoolers! One day they leave for school, and mothers are "free" again. There is probably no period in the family life cycle as confining as these early years. Small children require constant care and attention. It is a draining time for the best of parents. It is

also a time when there is so much to be learned, and parents are the primary teachers.

Besides these early years, there are other demanding times (as when they are teenagers) when it is well to remember: "This too shall pass." Sometimes parents think that if they have to drive their children to one more activity, they will perish. However, it will not last forever. Investing time and energy during these child-rearing years usually pays big dividends throughout the adult years of children.

WHAT CHILDREN NEED FROM PARENTS

We have just presented some guidelines for surviving as parents. However, most parents want to do more than merely survive: they want to live with joy and meaning as a family of parents and children. They want to live in ways that meet their needs and the needs of the children. There are many things children need from parents in order to grow into healthy, happy adults. The following seem important to us:

1. *Children need to be cared for physically.* In Maslow's hierarchy of needs, physical needs are considered basic.[25] That is, children's basic physical needs must be met before they are ready to meet other social and psychological needs.

Erikson emphasizes the significance of adequate physical care of the infant and small child as the prelude to the development of basic trust.[26] It is this basic trust which provides the secure foundations for life itself. Although we have been aware of the importance of meeting physical needs for many years, they continue to be just as necessary. Any list of children's needs must include the physical ones.

2. *Children need opportunities to feel good about themselves.* Having a healthy self-concept is something that most parents recognize as important. Parents play an important

role in its development. The original images that children have of themselves are formed in the family. This happens as family members respond to the children in ways that communicate that the children are valued (or not valued) as worthwhile, lovable, competent. That is, the children's self-concept is largely the product of how they perceive themselves as mirrored in the opinions and attitudes of others toward them. Negative ideas that children have about themselves change slowly and may persist for a lifetime.

What exactly is the role of parents in this development? The six-year study conducted by Stanley Coopersmith with preadolescent boys concerning self-esteem has some significant findings for parents. In essence, this study points out the need for parents to provide good models if high self-esteem is to be achieved by their children. They themselves should be developing and growing as persons exercising rights of their own. The Coopersmith study also suggests that it is beneficial for children to have firm and consistent boundaries that reflect the values of their parents, yet sufficient freedom to explore within these limits. Finally, parents desiring to encourage the development of high self-esteem should be knowledgeable of their children's worlds, their friends, their activities, and provide encouragement where needed.[27]

In addition to the above, one specific thing we think parents can do to help children develop healthy self-concepts is to aid them in discovering those things they do well—something they can feel good about as they express themselves as individual persons. (These are frequently activities the parents *cannot do!*) With our two children, playing musical instruments, involvement with Scouts, stamp collections, and learning self-expression through art forms played an important role during their preadolescent and adolescent development. Through these means they had chances to experience achievement and success. For others, it may have been sports or drama. All of these help children to feel good about themselves. Parents, in turn, can be highly supportive of them as they develop these skills. This gives structure to the development of self-worth and provides opportunities for growth.

3. *Children need firm and consistent guidelines and boundaries.* As noted in the Coopersmith study, children with high self-esteem tended to come from families that had firm guidelines and boundaries. (However, these were not rigid, as they permitted their children freedom to explore within this framework.) Knowing where the boundaries are helps give a child security; being able to make personal decisions within these boundaries helps develop independence and self-confidence.

Parents should also be consistent about enforcing these boundaries. If it is not acceptable for Junior to jump on the couch one day, it should also not be acceptable the next. However, as the child grows older, certain areas will require reevaluation and renegotiation. For example, the major issue with five-year-old Mary may be telling mother where she is going in the neighborhood to play. At seventeen, the issue may be that she return the car at the agreed-upon time after a football game.

4. *Children need parents who do not major in minors.* If parents are going to establish firm guidelines, they must determine what is most important to them as parents. Everything cannot be of major importance. If we consider that being a good student and driving safely are major areas for us, then we may need to place less emphasis on our personal preference for dress style. (The implications of poor grades and reckless driving to us are much more serious than dress style.) If it is important to us that our

children develop their skills (e.g., sports, music, drama), then we might occasionally have to close the door on a messy room. (We have never heard of a case of a "terminal messy room.") As important as it is for parents to make their priorities clear, the child must also have room for individual expression and choices within this framework.

We remember talking with a mother at a church conference on the family. It seemed that the most important thing to her at that time was how to get her son to clean his room. She also did not like the length of his hair. Beyond this, he was really a "good kid"—went to church, was a good student and not in trouble. However, this mother was about to destroy the relationship over the things he was doing that she did not like, even though he was being responsible in the areas she considered most important. She was a good example of majoring in minors.

It is important for us as parents to know where we want to draw the line; where we are willing to make exceptions; where we can give the necessary freedom that is required in growth toward independence. It may be that the most severe rejection going on between parents and children is in the areas that are really not that important. However, if the areas *really are important*, parents should "hold the fort."

5. *Children need to feel good about their bodies and appropriate sex information for their stage of development.* In the chapter on sex in this book we explored the importance of feeling comfortable "inside one's skin." Feeling good about our bodies (and sex in general) is probably more caught than taught. That is, parents inevitably communicate their attitudes toward the body and sex to the children in dozens of subtle ways. This suggests that perhaps the best way to ensure children's healthy attitudes toward themselves as sexual beings is to make sure we ourselves have healthy attitudes.

Sex education is not "just the facts." However, for the young child the facts are important. Sometimes we seem to think that once the facts have been presented, the job is over. It has really just begun! As children grow, conversations about their growing bodies are important. It is important to stay in touch with the child's feelings about sexuality. We also think it is important for children to know the significance of love and commitment in sexual expressions. Finally, discussions on how people manipulate and exploit others sexually are equally important.

6. *Children need experiences with their parents where there is quality time and a sense of "connectedness."* Time is measured in at least two dimensions—quantity and quality. Some parents may spend more time with their child than other parents, but there is little quality in it, since there is nothing much happening between the two of them (such as watching television together in the same room). Another parent may spend less time with the child but put more quality into it, since much is happening between the parent and child. (Of course, there are those busy parents who justify neglecting the child's need for parental attention by saying that they put quality into the time they do have. You can put only so much quality into a given amount of time, and the parent may in fact end up giving the child neither time nor quality!)

We suggest the following for evaluating the quality of the time you have with your child: Did you and your child really "connect" during your time together? Were you deeply aware of each other's presence? Were you experiencing a meeting of minds, or communion of spirits? Were you listening to each other with the whole person? Did you sense each other's uniqueness and a profound feeling of acceptance of these differences?

It doesn't appear to make a lot of difference what parents

and children do together in their quality time as long as there is some sense of connectedness. It could be a conversation together, or it may be the awareness your daughter has that up there somewhere in the bleachers you are rooting for her in an important gymnastic contest. These, we think, are some of the ingredients of quality time—of being connected. Many of them come naturally. Others have to be cultivated. These need not be the characteristics of every parent-child encounter, but, rather, provide goals for the overall relationship.

7. *Children need growing parents.* Evelyn M. Duvall believes that fathers and mothers who continue their growth as persons beyond their roles as parents do better in letting their children go to grow into adults themselves.[28] It is this "letting our children go" that is the ultimate goal of good parenting. When parents take time to continue growing, they are less likely to attempt to relive their lives through the children. They can be interested in the activities of their children, for the child's sake. If parents are taking care of their own identities, children have greater opportunities to develop theirs. In doing this, parents provide good role models. This is, perhaps, the best way to learn.

8. *Children need parents "to take delight" in them.* This is another way of saying that children need the affirmation that comes from knowing they are really wanted. What Sam Keen wrote about his father expresses what we desire to communicate concerning "delight taking" in our children. He wrote that living with his father was exciting, secure, and colorful. His father did all the things a father should do for his children, not the least of which was merely delighting in their existence.[29]

Once we become parents, falling into the pitfall of seeing life as all seriousness is such an easy one. Virginia Satir writes: "People play such cruel tricks on themselves when

Guidelines for Living with Children

they become parents. Suddenly now they must 'do their duty,' be serious, and give up lightness and joy. They can no longer indulge themselves, or even have fun."[30]

As we have noted in this chapter, living with children can be frustrating. Yet, for most of us our children are the source of some of our greatest joys and satisfactions. We began this chapter by saying that living with children is much like reading a novel—we enjoy the excitement and adventure, but we anxiously await the final outcome. If this chapter has helped you to be a little less anxious as you await the final "chapter" in your children's development, then we have been successful. In the meanwhile, relax. They will likely turn out to be decent people. After all, you turned out to be a reasonably competent person despite *your* parents' fears!

5
Relating to the Other Generation

Relating to the generation just older and the one younger than ourselves is a lifelong task. It is seldom accomplished without a certain degree of uncertainty, hesitation, and conflict for all parties concerned. All of this was brought home to us personally in recent years as we became aware that our children were now young adults, out of the nest, and wanting and needing us to relate to them differently. With the marriage of our son, this was further complicated by our suddenly becoming in-laws, a role to which we were unaccustomed. This also changed the relationship with our son, who then became a husband in a family separate from ours. Neither they nor we had much experience with the dependent-independent issues attendant at the launching of a new family. We have coped with this on a trial-and-error basis using a good communication network to keep the system in balance.

While the two of us have been learning to relate to the younger generation, we have also been "shifting gears" learning how to relate to the generation ahead of us—aging parents. Their ages and health mean they are becoming increasingly dependent upon us. Again, dependent-independent issues are a certain concern for both ourselves and our aging parents.

As if this were not enough, while all of this was going on, we became aware that the leaving of the children had thrown our marriage into a new transition. During the child-rearing years, we discovered, we had in some measure lost contact and now had to rediscover each other. (Discovering each other in your forties is quite different from doing so in your twenties!) Since the children no longer needed as much of her attention, Juanita found herself asking questions about her identity and purpose in life with an intensity not experienced since adolescence. By this time Wallace was also well into his career and wrestling with what he calls the "middle age uneasies." That is, he was not at all unhappy with his work, but on the other hand he was not sure he wanted to do "more of the same" for the next twenty years. The result was a kind of existential uneasiness. So while we have been trying to relate to the younger generation and the aging generation, we have also been learning to cope with more distinctly personal issues as well as working out a new relationship with each other. It's enough to make you tired!

In this chapter we want to look at relating to the other generation from three vantage points: from the standpoint of newly marrieds relating to middle-aged parents; from the standpoint of the middle-aged relating to both their married children and their aging parents; and from the vantage point of aging parents relating to their middle-aged children. Our goal is that, whatever your stage of life might be, this will facilitate the exploration of relating to the other generations in your life.

The Newly Married

The wisdom of the ages states that in marriage a person must "leave father and mother." Having left their parents, the two persons must now cling to their mates. If one of the major developmental tasks of adolescence has been accomplished, that of separating oneself from parents in order to establish personal identity, then the leaving part of this ancient truth has already been put into motion, though perhaps not completed. This will make clinging to each other for the newly married easier to accomplish, although not without difficulty. It is more difficult for some because they have never taken the first step toward leaving father and mother. In this respect, they may be more like adolescents than adults. Or, if they have never separated from parents sufficiently to establish their own identities, then the mate may become the "new" father or mother.

Then, again, there may be the newly married man or woman who finds that he or she possesses the needed skills to relate to his or her own parents on a mature level, but does not know what to do with the in-laws. Relating to in-laws is a major topic of concern with the newly married. It is an understandable concern and problem because couples must make the difficult transition from being unmarried members of the family into which they were born, to being members of enlarged family circles that come ready-made with the wedding.[31] To be more specific, most research suggests that it is the wife who more often thinks in-laws are a problem, and her feelings are usually directed toward her husband's mother.[32]

How important are these in-law relationships? A study of 544 student couples in the first year of marriage revealed a close relationship between a good adjustment in marriage and getting along with in-laws.[33] That is, a good relationship with the in-laws is usually predictive of a good marital adjustment. In fact, it was found that if the marriage failed in the first year, the problem most often listed as the cause for the failure was the in-law problem. It was also found that the younger the bride, the more frequently couples reported disagreements with their in-laws.[34] Howard Hovde found in his study that most parents want to be good in-laws, but simply do not know how.[35] How does one express love and interest without risking meddling?

Part of the difficulty may be that American newlyweds start a new family with so few resources. Margaret Mead writes that "very few human societies, other than ours, have encouraged young people to start a new family with such small backing from parents and wider kin group."[36] Young couples today are expected and expect to exercise much independence, unlike earlier times when parental help was generally accepted. Roof-raisings and housewarmings were common in pioneer days, and it was not unusual to find families living and working together under one roof on the farm.

Not only do those conducting research in the area of relating to in-laws today suggest that it is not wise to live under the same roof, some think it is better to live in different cities. Judson and Mary Landis found that if a young couple can live some distance away from both families, the partners probably have an advantage in establishing a good adjustment in their own marriage.[37] This is especially helpful in the first year of marriage. After some time together on their own without too much contact with parents, young couples usually find relationships with parents easier to establish on a mature level.

We are aware of the fact that relating to in-laws is indeed a problem, or that it can be. You, as a young couple, may be saying: "This we know, but what can we do about better relationships?" Just knowing doesn't make the problem any easier. For this reason, we make the following suggestions in the hope that they will aid you in relating to the other generation in ways that may be growth-producing.

1. Remember that your in-laws are people, too, and should be treated with the same courtesy, thoughtfulness, and respect that you would treat other important people in your lives.

2. Remember that your in-laws, like yourselves, are having to learn how to relate in this new relationship. This takes time. Be patient with them.

3. Remember that if you ask advice of your in-laws, you have in effect invited them to become involved in your personal lives. If you do not want this, do not ask for advice.

4. If in-laws offer advice or suggestions, treat this with the same kind of consideration that you would give to advice and suggestions from others. Do not "consider the source," and dismiss it summarily. If it is good advice, heed it; if poor, ignore it.

5. When you visit in-laws, make your visits brief. You will have to determine how long is "too long" in your family.

6. If you live in the same city, you will have to establish additional guidelines regarding visiting. We believe that in your first year of marriage, visits should not be too frequent. This may need to be openly talked about with the mate and parents.

7. Be friends with your in-laws, but do not neglect to develop friends with your own peer group.

8. If you and your mate have difficulties, it is probably wisest not to complain to the in-laws. Find someone who can be more objective.

9. Insofar as possible, it is best to establish your own autonomy apart from your in-laws. This means living in your own home, and not accepting substantial amounts of financial aid from them.

10. Finally, do not hesitate to seek professional help if your in-laws are a source of continuing concern.

Relating to in-laws is not the only adjustment a young couple must make. While working on relationships with your parents, you will also need to keep in mind the following adjustmental areas. Being aware of these may encourage you to not blame parents and in-laws for every problem you have. (However, we are aware that problems have a way of becoming interrelated.)

In addition to concerns with your parents and in-laws, we want to note the following other adjustmental areas: First, you are learning what it means to be a husband or a wife. This is a new role to you. What it means to be a husband in his family may be quite different from what it means in her family. Thus, there is a clash of role expectations. Secondly, you are working out a process for decision-making. Scores of decisions must be made. Which ones does he make, which ones does she make, which ones do they make together? What do they do when they disagree? Thirdly, you are working on how to handle feelings in your new family. Some are rather open with feelings; others rather reserved. Some let anger out and this can paralyze certain mates who are unused to such expressions of hostility. You may also find that expression of affection after marriage is rather different from during courtship. (What passed for affection then may have been merely passion.) Fourthly, you will be working on establishing a meaningful sexual relationship. Finally, you will be facing a multitude of problems related to money. Your greatest need for money is often just as you are establishing your family, and your income then is usually at its lowest. Money is often reported to be the major area of conflict for young marrieds.

All of this helps us to understand that being newly married is a full-time job. It is a big transition from leaving father and mother to establishing a new family, independent of the one in which you grew up, and yet having sufficient maturity and skills to relate meaningfully to those who love you and whom you also love.

Mid-Life Couples

If you are in the middle years, have a newly married son or daughter, and have read the chapter up to this point, we, the authors, may be in trouble! You may have felt attacked! You don't see yourself as such a problem. We understand your concern. In fact, we can identify with these feelings, since, as stated earlier, we too are in-laws to the newly married.

We are also aware that we are the "caught" generation—right in the middle. Those in mid-life are attempting to relate to growing and maturing children on the one hand, and trying to deal creatively with aging parents on the other hand. At the same time, middle age itself is such an important stage of life. There is much personal growing to be done in this critical time for marriages. Divorce among our middle-aged acquaintances has become much more commonplace. After twenty or more years of marriage a growing number are "throwing in the towel."

Since we devoted space to the newly marrieds' problems of relating to in-laws, we will deal first with this issue here. Then we want to look at the special opportunities the middle-aged have to grow as persons, and at the same time protect themselves from an overinvestment of emotional energy with the other generations.

With regard to the in-law issue, we think it is best to face it squarely. It requires skill to handle it properly; no one does a perfect job. If a father has been a possessive parent, he does not change this overnight just because his daughter got married. If a mother has a tendency to dominate, her son's or daughter's wedding ceremony will not stop that. However, if she continues to dominate, the only thing this will likely now bring her married son or daughter is trouble! These are not make-believe problems. They are real! They are not only disturbing for the newly married, they can make life miserable for the parents, too. It can especially make life miserable for the daughter-in-law and the mother-in-law in whose relationship the trouble is most often found.

What can parents do? They should do anything but build their lives around the new marriages of their children. One of life's great rewards is "making it on your own." Parents of the newly married need often to remind themselves of this. Many of us like to get together and compare stories of our struggles to get through school, to set up our first home, to get our first new car, or to purchase our first house. But we, the current middle-aged generation, do not want our children to struggle. Yet it is out of these struggles that firm bonds are made and strength forged. We may still be blaming the Depression, wars, our early poverty; or we simply want to share what we have while we are still alive. All of these may be good reasons for the middle-aged parent. However, it is not in the best interests of our children to deny them the right to make it on their own. (When parents feel guilty for not giving more financial help to their children, it may be well to remember the above sentence.)

This letting go of children, even when they are married, is not easy. We cannot deny the impact it has on parental lives. However, if parents and children do not work on it, the relationship may lead to abrupt "ripping apart." Letting go is important because mid-life couples cannot deal creatively with their own stage in life if they cling to a past one. They need to remember that new possibilities will come into their lives now that their children have moved out on their own. Eda LeShan, in an excellent book on the middle years, believes that this is one of the richest and most creative stages of life. In fact, she states that this is the time individuals can make conscious choices more clearly and strongly than ever before, because we know much about ourselves.[38]

It is so easy to fall into the trap that leads us to spend all our emotional energy fretting about our relationships rather than dealing creatively with them. Part of the reason some of us get nowhere is that "knowing ourselves," noted above, does not come automatically. For this reason, some never become skilled in this inner life. (Getting in touch with our feelings is another way of experiencing the inner life.) Facing ourselves as we really are is not something everyone accomplishes. However, it is something that everyone who is growing accomplishes. Growing requires that we take a careful look at where we have been, where we are, and where we want to go. This begins to give us new purpose. As Gail Sheehy reminds us in *Passages*: "If we have confronted ourselves in the middle passage and found renewal of purpose around which we are eager to build a more authentic life structure, these may well be the best years."[39]

Erik Erikson wrote much of the pivotal material that helps with understanding life's stages. The major task of men and women in mid-life, he says, is to answer for themselves three basic questions: (1) What is really important to me; who are the people for whom I care the most? (2) What is it that I can do well? (3) And how do I plan to carry off what I have started and created in life?[40] He called this generativity. This means a desire to care for others in the broadest sense. Erikson believes that at mid-life we need to move out of ourselves and be more concerned with giving of ourselves to worthwhile causes and caring for others—if we want to grow. But the concept of generativity also includes being more productive and creative. It means taking our total selves and making a creative investment of care and love in persons and worthwhile causes. Robert Coles believes that essentially generativity comes down to the real test of all love and asks the question: "Do we *care* enough to offer anything to others?"[41]

What we are doing is presenting a case for making these middle years creative ones. As emphasized, if emotional energy is continually and grudgingly invested out of proportion to the other generations in the family, this important stage of life may not reach its rich potential. This is the time of life when we can free ourselves from the rigidity of prescribed caring relationships (with children, parents, siblings) to strive for this caring, "because we want to," for others in the broadest sense. This generativity can be liberating. It can also free us to care for our family members in ways that are meaningful rather than just being prescribed and demanding.

What happens if we do not generate? The alternative, Erikson believes, is to stagnate. If a person stagnates as an individual, we can be assured that all other relationships will also stagnate. We are especially concerned for what this might do to the marriage. Just as personal growth does not come automatically, neither does growth for the marriage.

One of the reasons why enriching marriage in the middle years is difficult is that many couples are unaware that such enrichment is possible, or even necessary. From our own experience in both participating in and leading many marriage enrichment groups, we have learned some things that have helped us grow in these middle years. When you are tempted to think that the only reason you were put on the earth was to worry about your children or to be overly concerned with your parents, think about the following list. Better still, make a list of your own.

1. *Grow as persons.* This could mean taking a university class, joining a book club, making a new friend, trying your hand at writing, or taking a class in auto mechanics. You will have to decide what is growth-producing for you. However, do not depend on your job to provide the motivation for growth; the ruts there may be too deep for you to change directions where needed.

2. *Get out of the house as a couple.* This may sound trite, but we think it will work. It may not be good economic advice to suggest that you get into your car, drive two or more miles to a donut shop for a cup of coffee, but it can be a good marriage investment.

3. *Keep each other informed* as to the changes you are experiencing in these middle years. (This is what you talk about over coffee at the donut shop—not the children and elderly parents.) You can be assured that the middle years will bring change. It can be exciting if shared, or it can cripple the marriage if it becomes a private journey.

4. *Get involved in a worthwhile project.* Do it together if possible. It may be a project for the larger community. You may have been doing this all your married life. However, this time do it differently. Make sure you are not mainly concerned with controlling what is happening; let meeting your needs be secondary; and don't be concerned about who gets the credit for what is accomplished—especially if you think it is you. This is one of the rewards of middle

age—doing something for someone else "for the simple joy of doing something for someone else."

In conclusion, those in the middle years may have to ask themselves many times, "What is really important to me?" This may call for a reevaluation of priorities. The reassessment of personal values in mid-life may be one of the greatest aids for relating more effectively to the other generation.

Elderly Parents

In one week's time, three different persons talked with us at length about their concerns with elderly parents. Relating to aging parents is something most of those in the middle years are facing, or will soon face. Some do it reasonably well. But for others, it is a time of extreme stress and anxiety. Deep rifts in family ties often occur, growing out of disagreements over how to care for an aging parent. However, under the best of circumstances, it is a difficult time of life for all concerned.

In doing research for this part of the chapter, we were struck by the fact that many books seem addressed directly to young people, single people, married people, but books concerned with the aging are quite another story. For some reason, authors do not address books to the elderly as an audience. Rather, we write *about* older people. Of course, there is some justification for doing this. The elderly are not likely to be reading the book anyway. Or perhaps since the middle-aged are most often the ones looking for information concerning aging parents, they seem to be the most appropriate audience to address. However, though the practice may be justified, what this sometimes does is make us see the elderly as less than persons and miss seeing them as unique individuals in their own important stage of life. We miss something of value, it seems to us, if we only speak *about* them and do not let them at times speak *to* us and *for* themselves. Though we address ourselves in this part of the chapter to middle-aged people who are concerned with aging parents, we will draw heavily on what the elderly have said on the subject. We want them to speak for themselves.

Fortunately, a few good books are now available on the subject of aging written by older people themselves, some beyond seventy. Dorothy Fritz, one such writer beyond seventy, has written a book designed to help those who are younger to understand what it is like being an older person. She expresses particular concern about sweeping generalizations that are often made about the elderly, and the grim, cold facts with which they are sometimes described. Regarding the problems of the aging she says:

> Of course, all elderly people have problems, but so have preschoolers. Of course, some elderly people are difficult to deal with. But is this not true of adolescents and young adults? Of course, the aging and aged are often pessimistic and negative. But is this not also true of those in middle age who see the years slipping away with their dreams, ideals, and goals, unfulfilled?[42]

Seeing the elderly as persons seems to be an important theme woven throughout the books written by the elderly. This theme is picked up by Paul Tournier, who, writing in his seventies, reminds us:

> If an old man sees that you are really interested in his personal life, you will see a wonderful transformation take place in him. Just like the child, the old man needs to be spoken to and

listened to in order to become a person, to become aware of himself, to live and grow. You will have brought about something that no social service can do of itself: you will have promoted him to the rank of person.[43]

When thinking of the elderly, both of us immediately recall a group of about forty retired persons, many well beyond seventy, whom we were with in a church family enrichment conference in Texas. These, we discovered, were forty highly individualistic, thinking persons. One in his eighties had gone back to college and received a master's degree. Another had recently written a book. All were articulate and alert. What do you say to a group like this? We did not try, but let them talk to us. Among other things, they had many thoughts and feelings about their children trying to relate to them as "children." When we left that group we felt refreshed and more optimistic about getting older ourselves. We have never met with a group that seemed livelier and happier.

Most elderly persons are not willing to "put on the shawl and head for a rocking chair." The activity schedule of many would make the much younger weary. In her book *Growing Old Is a Family Affair*, Dorothy Fritz makes a long list of things that her friends over seventy are doing. It includes teaching neighborhood boys to use tools, tutoring schoolchildren, leading a children's choir, and helping in a hospital.[44]

Up to this point we have attempted to establish the individual personhood of the aging. We have sought to do away with the myth that all elderly persons are alike—needing to be watched over by others. One book gives us this information:

> Despite popular belief, most persons adjust quite well to the changes in their lives. Your parents may be in the adaptable majority. Old age by itself is not a problem. It is the final stage in the cycle of living. Most men and women over 65 are healthy enough to carry on their normal activities—only 15 percent are not. Less than 5 percent of the elderly are in institutions, nursing homes for the aged at any one time.[45]

When we are one generation attempting to relate to another—in this instance elderly parents—what are some of the things to be remembered? Andrew and Judith Lester suggest that "we must walk that narrow path between being overprotective of our parents and being unconcerned or ignorant.[46] Going to either extreme could be (for lack of a better term) a cop-out. A person might make unilateral decisions concerning parents "in their [the parents'] best interest." Or a person might say, "Mom and Dad have managed fine for eighty years; they certainly don't need me to hold their hand just because the years are coming on."

We are certainly aware that decisions sometimes have to be made, along with the parents, concerning problems in their futures. Taking time to give it our best consideration and attention makes a difference in how things will work out. One of us (Juanita) will relate the personal journey of her mother as it became a family affair, and provided opportunity for us all to grow in our relationships to each other.

At age seventy-eight my mother, like many of the elderly, was the victim of great deal of loss in her life. My father had been dead fifteen years, and when she was sixty-eight my only brother and family moved from the town where she lived. Her closest friend of many years died of a

Relating to the Other Generation

heart attack while they were out shopping together. Her brothers and sisters, like herself, were getting old, and lived across the state. I, her only daughter, was living 800 miles away. We talked about all of this at length in the summer of her seventy-seventh year. I asked her to think, during the coming year, about selling her home and moving into an apartment in the town where we live. (She immediately liked the idea of having a place of her own in which to live.)

During the year following this conversation, we talked on the phone often about this possible move. I sent her pictures of places where she might live. I talked with her about what life in an apartment might be like; there would be new noises but less worry with upkeep. I wrote telling her we were really looking forward to her coming to be with us. Taking time to do this was important. I think she had a sense of thinking the matter through, then making her own decision. So, a year later, when she was seventy-eight, at her request, her home was sold and she moved into an apartment about four blocks down the street from our house. She expressed that it made her feel more secure moving to a new community if we were nearby.

I thought it was especially important that she make this move while she was still able to get out, meet people, and feel more a part of her new community. Also, I thought that if she were close by, and could be checked on by one of us in the family, she could live independently as long as possible for her remaining years. I discovered just how important this daily check is, when one day this year (she is now eighty) I telephoned her, and, receiving no answer, rushed to her apartment and found her in a coma. She was back home from the hospital in three days, and happy again to be in her own apartment—which she says is like home "because it has my furniture in it!" I learned one important thing from this: whereas I had checked on her before only in the evening, she should now also receive a phone call each morning as well. This was the only change, at this stage, that we had to make.

Another important help in her adjustment is my insistence that on weekends she phone friends she left behind. On Saturdays and Sundays, she would, and still does, work her way through the list. Phone calls were her main contact with them, even when she lived nearby. It is a small financial investment to aid in her adjustment.

These may appear to be small matters, but I searched for ways that would enable her in some way to find things in our larger city that were more like the things "at home" in her smaller town. For instance, I selected a pharmacist for her who seemed to take a personal interest in her health (as the one did at home). I found a physician for her near the age of the one she was accustomed to. Even though it was across the city, I took her to a beauty parlor where the operators seemed to relate to her not only as a person but as an important one. And, even though it would be simpler for me to purchase her groceries myself from her list, I make sure each week she has plenty of time to wander up and down the aisles, selecting those things she personally wants (and having an opportunity to express to me how expensive everything is getting).

One of the more significant things we discovered about my mother was that mail, paperwork, banking, red tape were the things that seemed to bother her most. It was a great relief for her when Wallace became her "business manager," handling, for example, the endless and confusing array of forms after she came home from the hospital. We became aware that such things must have created a great deal of anxiety for her before she moved and when she had no help from anyone.

I think my mother is happy with this dramatic move in

Relating to the Other Generation

her life. She left a few friends, but she has family to put in their places. I realize that if my father were still living, things would have been handled differently. I also realize that it is important for the members of each family to make what they think are good decisions for their situation. I had to deal with some persons who said they thought it was a shame my mother has to live by herself when we have empty bedrooms in our house. Little did they realize that having her "own place" was about the most important thing in her life. After my mother returned from the hospital, another person confronted me with the fact that she thought she should be put in a nursing home. (This person had just put her mother in a nursing home, and was apparently working out part of this grief on others.) At any rate, the point being made is, make your decisions with the aid of your parents, and stick by them. Both generations will be happier. Some parents may refuse any kind of change. You will, of course, have to handle your own situation.

Sure, relating to the other generation is not always easy. A full-time job makes a lot of demands on my time. Sometimes I do not have the time to do all the things I need to do. Sometimes I lose my patience. Even get angry. However, even in doing this, my mother is assured that I see her as a person—someone significant enough to merit anger, not just pity.

As in all relationships, sometimes things go smoother than at other times. This is certainly true when relating to elderly parents. An illness can come so quickly. It can demand so much. As one book observes:

> If you are involved with an elderly mother whose needs take up a lot of your time, your husband (or wife) and your children may give you great support, or resentment. They may

share your problems, or add to them. Your conflicting loyalties may sometimes be unbearable.[47]

Guilt may be another big factor in relating to elderly parents. Your relationship may never have been good, and being old doesn't change this. But if you have done what seems best for all concerned, you need not feel guilty.

There may be no easy way to get around these and other difficulties. However, as much as possible, it might be well for couples to discuss the avenues of care they might provide in different stages of their parents' needs. Financial resources are a factor in the kind of health care a family can provide. Looking in advance into medical insurance, and the care facilities this covers, would be better than waiting until a crisis comes. Even checking on possible nursing homes, making visits to them, and evaluating them can be done more easily before they are needed. If they are not needed, you have at least become acquainted with the kind of good or bad care other elderly persons in your community are receiving.

Another kind of information that might be helpful is, as one book suggests, to "think of the elderly in three separate groups." The first group is the young-old (up to 74), the middle-age old (75 to 85), and the old-old (85 and over).[48] The needs of the aging may be very different in each of these stages. If ill health makes it impossible for a person to manage independently, chronological age will be less important. However, it is important to remember that at each stage the elderly can bring more diversity than we sometimes realize. The kind of life a parent can live at seventy-five will likely be quite different at eighty-five.

In conclusion, the emotional demands on one generation relating to another should not become unreasonable. If these demands have gotten out of balance, whether that means a newly married couple spend more time in anger over in-laws than they do in joy in their own relationship, or a middle-age couple seem to be willing to sacrifice their marriage for an ill parent, it is not good. No one gains in these kinds of relationships. Everyone loses! However, as in all relationships, especially those with our other generations, there is as much potential for growth as for stagnation. Much of it will depend on what we really prefer, and what we intend to do about it.

6
Friendship: Source of Personal and Family Strength

Friendship has magically transforming qualities. A lowly hamburger shared with a friend becomes a banquet! A song shared with a friend becomes a concert! A friend's simple gift becomes a valued treasure! A friend's hug heals life's wounds! But without friendship, a hamburger is just a hamburger; a song just a song; a gift just a gift; and a hug just a hug. But mix that wondrous ingredient of friendship, and each of these becomes a momentous occasion.

For instance, not long ago we and six of our closest friends decided that our families would go camping in the spring before we scattered for the summer. We agreed to meet at a state park, but from the beginning things went wrong. All of us were late; some quite late. One family forgot tent stakes! (Ever try to drive twigs into rocky soil?) Another forgot sleeping bags! Then the rains started, and it appeared that the Great Flood was going to be reenacted. It rained as we ate, rained as we slept, rained as we arose in the morning. Everything was wet, including some sleeping bags. (Once wetness gets warm, it isn't too bad, though.) We huddled under postage-stamp-sized tarpaulins with feet firmly planted in cold, muddy pools of water. Numerous trips were made to the showers to wash the children, just to

Friendship: Source of Personal and Family Strength

see whose child still breathed beneath the mud!

Given just this information, you might conclude we had a miserable time. Wrong! We had a great time! In fact, as we departed that place of wet, muddy adventure, we agreed that it had been such a meaningful time that we wanted to repeat it each subsequent year no matter how far our families might get scattered across the country. How can you account for the transformation of "misery" into a joyous occasion of celebration? Friendship! We simply enjoy talking and being together, regardless of the circumstances.

These are some of the friends who have stood with us in our crises, and we with them. They are friends who have helped nurture our children; friends with whom we worship on Sundays; friends who listen to us; friends who affirm us by their very friendship. They are friends with whom we have worked, sung, laughed, and told ghost stories around the embers of a campfire. They know us well, but like us anyway! We accept each other! They are much like us, yet so very different from us. They are some of our most intimate friends, and when our next crisis or victory occurs, one of them will likely be the first we will tell.

A minister friend strongly recommends that couples whom he marries take steps to develop close friendships with other similar couples in the church, or from someplace. This is sound advice. We believe that close friendships with other couples who have basically satisfying relationships are one of the main bulwarks available to us against the forces of darkness that fragment and destroy modern marriages.

The research of Carle Zimmerman and Lucius Cervantes is relevant to this point.[49] In their little-known study of nearly 60,000 "successful American families," they concluded that the major key to their success lay in the fact that each family surrounded itself with friendship ties to four or five other families. These families formed their most intimate friendships and were also basically stable, "successful," and similar to themselves in age, background, religion, and ethical values. The adults spent much of their leisure time together, and their children often played together. Zimmerman and Cervantes believe that this network of four or five other family friendships provided a "nested" environment supplying emotional support and making it easier for them to pass on values they consider important to their children.

The counterpart of this grows out of our observation from working with troubled families who often report that their friends' marriages are in as bad shape as theirs. One of the things we sometimes do is attempt to get the couple to develop new friends with at least one couple who basically have their feet on the ground and their marital heads on straight! We believe that health is contagious, just as surely as sickness.

The subject of friendship, of course, is not a new one. Since ancient times, the nature and significance of friendship has been a topic explored by writers both great and small. C. S. Lewis notes: "To the Ancients, friendship seemed the happiest and most fully human of all loves; the crown of life and the school of virtue."[50] Aristotle devoted two chapters in *Nicomachean Ethics* to the subject of friendship. Much of what he wrote is as current as today's research of the subject. He described friendships as being necessary and natural. They imply some likeness between the persons involved. Around 360 B.C., he was using phrases such as "Like seeks like" and "Birds of a feather flock together." In fact, much of what has been written on friendship in recent years was first said by Aristotle centuries earlier.

Although Francis Bacon had few friends, he nevertheless wrote some beautiful passages concerning the subject of friendship. Ralph Waldo Emerson also concluded that: "Friendship, like the immortality of the soul, is too good to be believed." All these references from literature help to underline the importance of friendship as a topic of serious concern across the centuries. However, it is not a subject that has recently received the attention given to it by these early writers. Perhaps the modern world ignores it, as C. S. Lewis believes, because so few value it. And the reason so few value it, he suggests, is because so few have experienced it.[51]

In his book *Psychotherapy: The Purchase of Friendship*, William Schofield writes that twentieth-century Western culture has lost the close sharing friendships of older, less urbanized communities. That is, he believes that as modern families have moved from small communities where they lived surrounded by relatives and lifelong friends to the anonymity of large cities, they lost the natural listening posts of small communities. Therefore, the only viable alternative for some in the isolation of urban life is to "purchase" a friend—a psychotherapist.[52]

Why do we, the authors of this book, consider the topic of friendship a significant one for a book on marriage and family growth? Through our own experiences of personal growth and nurturing our family, we value it. If we did not value it personally, studies like the one cited earlier by Zimmerman and Cervantes would certainly make us want to consider it. In addition, as therapists, we have observed time and time again the positive impact of good friendships on the well-being of couples and families. So we not only value it, but we value it highly. Like Emerson, we have sometimes thought that good friends were too good to be true. This goodness has added immeasurable dimensions to our own joy as a family.

When we began to deal with this subject, we were impressed with its many dimensions. How can we do justice to the many facets of friendship? There are the friends we had as children. Friends Wallace has known since college days. Other friends Juanita has known independently of Wallace. Those whom we have known together. Some who have been special to our children. Others who have moved away, and we see them much less than we would like. Friendship is a big subject!

In the remainder of the chapter, we want to examine friendship in three ways. First, we will look at the kinds of friends that contribute to a person's growth as an individual. For instance, Juanita thinks of those occasions for growth with a friend she has met on a weekly basis for breakfast for seven years; Wallace thinks of a friend whom he does not see as frequently as he would like, but upon meeting, finds they are bound with the same trust and understanding that was there when they last met.

Secondly, we will write of those friends who become friends to the family; they become like "family." With so many in our day being far away from relatives, these friends soon slip quietly into these family spots and nurture us in special ways. They become our intentional family. We want to consider ways to develop this concept more fully.

Thirdly, we will take a look at some of the nitty-gritty aspects of deep friendships. Many people know how to make friends much better than how to keep them. Others do not know how to either make or keep them. We will explore some important considerations for the making and keeping of friends.

Friends and Individual Growth

One way we come to know ourselves and experience growth is through friendships. There is a compelling desire to know ourselves and be known by another that makes friendships so important. Someone recognizes her voice coming from another room. Another can tell who is approaching by his walk. Or she might say, "It has your special touch." In *The Little Prince*, the author illustrates this specialness through a conversation between the fox and the little prince about friendship. In one passage, the fox says to the little prince: "To me, you will be unique in all the world. To you, I shall be unique in all the world. . . . I shall know the sound of a step that will be different from all the others."[53]

Lewis suggests and we ask, Is this kind of friendship a lost art? Many people do not know what we are referring to when we speak of uniqueness in friendships. Ask them to think of their friends, and the persons who come to mind may be no more than casual acquaintances. Hugh Black's small book, *Friendship*, written at the turn of the century, amusingly illustrates this point: "She that asks her dear five hundred friends cannot expect the exclusive affection, which she has not given." He comments further saying that the most common mistake we make is that we spread our friendship over too many people and have no "depth of heart left."[54]

Even Aristotle addressed this point. He believed that "it is as impossible to be friends with a great number of people in the purest sense of friendship, as it is to be in love with a great number of people at once." But he stated that it is possible to find a great number of acquaintances who are simply useful or pleasant or agreeable; for people of this kind are numerous and their services do not take much time. Therefore, the economy of time permits us to have only a few friends with the kind of closeness we are referring to here.

We know some people who are unusually gifted in making friends, and this skill enables them to have many friends. However, demands for the proper care of such friendships can take a toll on other aspects of their lives. These people may have little emotional energy left for their families. Their work may suffer. Or, because they are such giving people (a quality of those who have many friends) their own emotional resources may become depleted. They may give much more than they are receiving. Eventually, some become angry because so many people expect so much from them. So we are reminded once again that it is not wise for a person to try to have the largest number of intimate friends possible, since apparently no one can be a devoted friend to that many people at once.

When considering friendship, someone might ask: "Is one's mate one's friend?" We certainly hope so. Joel Block, however, found that in his random sample of two thousand couples only one third reported this to be so.[55] Friendship as we are referring to it here primarily has to do with friends other than one's spouse. Also, the person who claims only the mate as a friend is putting impossible demands on the marriage, since the mate cannot meet all of one's friendship needs. Most of us are complex persons with many needs. Many of us live far away from parents, brothers, sisters, and others who may be in our intimate circle. For a woman to expect her husband to meet all her emotional needs not only puts strain on their relationship, it could become boring after a few years of marriage. Good friendships bring enrichment to good marriages! These friendship relationships help us grow as individuals, then as couples.

Martin Marty notes: "Being open to friends breaks exclusiveness so that married people can rejoin the human race and be of service to others."[56]

As stated, one of the reasons that good friends are so important to us is that they help us to come to know ourselves more fully. Being understood by another is one way we deepen our awareness of ourselves. Tournier describes it this way: "No one can find a full life without feeling understood by at least one person. Misunderstood, he loses his self-confidence, he loses his faith in life, or even in God. . . . He who would see himself clearly must open up to a confidant freely chosen and worthy of such trust."[57]

We recognize the uniqueness of friends with those qualities which can contribute to our personal growth through their deep understanding of us. Juanita can name quickly the number of friends she has that fit this description. Wallace has the same experience, but believes it is not necessary that a person have a great number of friends of this quality. Two or three friends who *really* understand us may be enough. We also discover, when taking inventory of these close friends, that there is a lot of variety among them. Some we have known for many years, others only a short time. Some live nearby, others far away. They also come from several backgrounds. For both of us, our deepest friendships include both men and women.

We have personally always enjoyed sharing these close friends that we have as individuals (opposite sex, or same sex) with the rest of the family, when it is possible to do so. In fact, when a person—male or female—becomes really important to us, one way for that friendship to become secure over the years is to give it roots within the family system. This does not mean that the family group will share the same depth of friendship, the way friends might in a one-to-one experience, but the entire family can certainly benefit by coming to know someone who is so special to one of its members. Juanita remembers having a good friend say to her that one of the ways to give deep expression to a devoted friendship is by developing a loving and caring concern for that person's entire family. In this way all the family can enjoy the rewards of good friendships.

In summary, we have noted that our closest friends are few in number, understand us as individual persons, and through this understanding help us to grow. We have made a point of the fact that these friendships are special. Later in the chapter, we will discuss ways to nurture these close friendships that have come our way.

Growing Through Family Friendships

We want to move from a discussion of friendships as they relate to us primarily as individuals to a consideration of family friends. These individual friends may or may not become related to the entire family. However, there are those families who become friends to us as a family. These are the kinds of friends we referred to at the beginning of the chapter when we recounted the camping trip. There are certain families with whom we surround ourselves to help nurture our children, care for us in our griefs, celebrate our joys with us, and give us personal rootage in much of the impersonalness we find around us.

For us our approach to these family relationships has been informal. That is, we did not follow any kind of plan in developing these friends. However, for those interested in a more formal approach, Margaret Sawin has developed material for organizing such families. She refers to these groups as "family clusters," where four or five families contract with each other to form a support group. They meet monthly, or as frequently as they desire, and a program is planned to meet specific family needs. These programs are designed to give mutual support to each other, training in relationship skills, and provide a time to celebrate their life and beliefs together.[58] Family clusters have been especially effective in church settings.

When we examine family relationships in our lives, we begin to notice some definite characteristics. As stated, it was for us something that developed naturally. At any given time, we have four or five families with whom we are close. We are not related to each family in the circle of friends in exactly the same way. There are one or two families with whom we share more deeply and with whom we have conversations at times when we are not together as a family group. One family we have known for fifteen years, others for six or eight, and others less than three years. In addition to these, we are friends of families whom we have known much longer, but they do not live in our community and thus are not a part of our daily lives. Also, there are some families with whom we used to be closer than we are now. For a variety of reasons, we grew apart. If friends no longer find their relationship meaningful, then it makes sense to move on—especially if this appears to be mutually agreeable.

There is something else significant about our family friendships. Over the years, we have been in and out of one another's homes. "Go often to the house of thy friend; for weeds soon choke up the unused path" is an old Scandinavian quotation that might well be our slogan. At times we go to a restaurant for dinner with these friends, but this is not the same as being in each other's homes. This is especially important for the children who are more involved in these home gatherings.

In many ways these friends become our "family"—or our intentional family. As with so many families, our relatives live several states away. So these friends become the "clan" that helps us celebrate a birthday, a graduation, or a special meal at Thanksgiving. They are in touch with what is happening with us. They are aware that our son has won a music award or they admire the pottery our daughter has made. All of this has helped our children feel important and affirmed by someone other than their parents. We believe family friends make a vital contribution to children's sense of worth and identity.

We may appear to be making a strong point of having friends in our homes, and going to theirs. We do think this is important. It is especially important during the child-rearing years. However, we are not suggesting that each of us should become the "hostess with the mostest." We are not thinking here about parties, big dinners, or giant productions. We are not suggesting that a family should have others over so often that it jeopardizes their need for family privacy. Privacy is important, too. As suggested above, we are more concerned with having around us on special occasions those four or five families to whom we are closely related.

These special families that come on special occasions provide the children with a bridge to the outside world. These families, Zimmerman and Cervantes found, help in the nurturing of the children by establishing a common value system.[59] When we share some concern regarding our child, these friends do not secretly take delight in it. It is one of these families that may provide a refuge of caring for our son or daughter when he or she is having trouble "getting through" to us. We know they will do this, because we will do the same for them.

These friends who contribute to the lives of our children sometimes go beyond the call of duty. We remember friends who no longer had children in the home going with us to the football games to watch our son perform with the band at halftime. We have gone to the senior play with other parents to watch their budding starlet perform on stage. Other friends have sat with us through a long evening of a student talent show, to finally hear our daughter sing at the close of the coffee house program. (As you can see, children in the family really test your friendships!) We could not purchase such important contributions to the lives of our children, for such interest and affirmation is more valuable than money.

Not all of our friends still have children in the home. We no longer do ourselves. This does not make family friends any less important. Even though our children are away, these friends have continuing ties with them. Also, we enjoy being a part of the lives of those friends of ours who still do have children in the home. It is satisfying to know that we can make a small contribution to something as exciting as a young and developing life. Our family friends also include those who are divorced or widowed and live alone. They seem to be especially gifted in not taking our friendship for granted. They make us feel good when they remind us how important we are to their lives. We learn from their graciousness.

Sometimes these close friends to our family move away. For most of us, this mobile society is not something we just read about in books on sociology, but is something we experience. There have been those moments when we felt like saying it is just not worth the effort. We pour out our energies in developing close friendships, and at the first chance they have for advancement, they leave us. Fortunately, such depth of despair is fleeting. True, these friends will not be a part of our daily lives, and consequently we are aware they will lose some of their significance. However, the investments for good they have made in our lives will always be there. They have increased our awareness of what makes a friendship good. They continue to serve as models for us as a family as we develop new friends. Kahlil Gibran helps us feel poetic about such partings:

> When you part with your friend, you grieve not;
> For that which you love most in him may be clearer in his absence, as the mountain to the climber is clearer from the plain.[60]

We are also reminded of the parting that Theodor Reik had with his close friend, Sigmund Freud, at their last meeting. To do justice to this beautiful passage, Reik should be quoted directly:

> I flew from Amsterdam to Vienna to say goodby to Freud. We both knew we would not see each other again. After we shook hands, I stood at the door and could not say a word. My lips were pressed together so hard they were unable to part. He must have sensed what I felt: he put his arm on my shoulder and said, "I've always liked you." (He had never before said anything of this kind.) As I bowed my head wordless, he said in a low but firm voice, as if to comfort me, "People need not be glued together when they belong together."[61]

Earlier we raised the question as to whether a husband and wife could be best friends and agreed that this is important, but outside the scope of this chapter. Related to that issue is one that closely parallels it; it has to do with close friendships between parents and their adult (and perhaps married) children. Of course, throughout history close relatives have often provided meaningful friendships. Many families today are aware of the meaningful relationships they have with their adult children, especially those who live in the same community. Many of these often eat together, go to social events together, and may even attend the same church.

There is no question that these bonds can be deeply meaningful. However, we think it is imperative that both the parents and the children also have close friends with their own peer group. We think it is particularly important for the young couple to have close friends with their own age group. At this stage they are in the process of establishing themselves as persons and a family separate and apart from their parents. Friendships with the parents to the exclusion of close friendships with their own peer group, we believe, can thwart young marrieds in accomplishing this vital goal. (This is covered in more detail in Chapter 5, "Relating to the Other Generation.")

Interestingly, Zimmerman and Cervantes rule out friendships with relatives as the ideal friendship. They believe such relationships tend to be "compulsive" and hence only imperfect friendships. Though relationships with relatives are usually friendly, they believe that their primary essence is status, not friendship.[62] That is, the relationship flows from the status of the other person as a relative rather than attraction based on personal qualities, as in a friendship. Friendship should be free. Martin Marty notes that friendship is one of the freest forms of association in most cultures. No one signs papers in friendships. It has to be given; no one can take it or demand it from you.[63]

In this section, we have attempted to look at the characteristics that are found in those friends who nurture our families. We have emphasized their importance in rearing our children. We have also suggested ways to strengthen the concept of "families ministering to families." We now want to move to a very practical dimension of this subject, and look at some of those nitty-gritty concerns in making and keeping friends.

MAKING AND KEEPING FRIENDS

For some people, making friends is easy. For others, it is nearly impossible. Some people make friends easily, but do not know how to keep them. People they have called "friends" may be more like acquaintances. No one, of course, can tell another person how to make a friend. People are too different. Needs vary from person to person. However, we think that there are certainly some things we can share about the qualities needed for making and keeping friends.

A person does not go shopping for a friend at some Friendship Mall. Even the fox knew better than this, when he said to the little prince: "Men have no more time to understand anything. They buy things all ready made at the shops. But there is no shop anywhere where one can buy friendship, and so men have no friends any more."[64] Friendship is not something one goes desperately searching for, as if it can be found and quickly purchased. At its very best, it moves toward depth slowly. This is why it requires time. This leads us to suggestions for some of the needed qualities we believe are important in making and keeping friends.

1. Recognizing the need for an *investment of time* is one of the first steps in moving toward deep friendships. We wrote earlier that once a person becomes aware of the amount of time needed to move from acquaintance to real friendship, the person will realize that one cannot nurture a great number of close friends at one time. Again, remember, we are writing about friendship as being something we find at our deeper level of existence. We are not necessarily

referring to that group of colleagues we might have over from the office, though they meet some of our needs; or the group of companions from the Sunday school class, though our friends may be in these groups.

2. *Availability* is another quality needed for the making and keeping of friends. We have friends where just a phone call asking, "Would you meet us at the donut shop for a cup of coffee?" means they will be there. Just as important, they call us to meet them, and we go. The fact that they call us makes us feel that our desire to be together is mutual. There have been others who caused us to feel as if we were being put on a waiting list when we attempted to work out a plan for some simple activity. We eventually discovered that what some of these families wanted was large groups of acquaintances, and did not desire (or perhaps understand) the level of friendship we were seeking.

3. *Making sure we are not taking our friends for granted* is another important quality in good friendships. Sometimes we need to stop and take stock of our relationships. In doing this, we may discover some friends who have gone out of their way to nurture us. We cannot remember when we did something special for them. It is not that we do not enjoy doing for them, or being with them. We really do! But if we made the same kind of investment in their lives that they have made in ours, we would have to give up some of the valuable time in our busy schedules. In this friendship we may have become only receivers; our friends are givers. (Giving is important, because it is one important way we grow as persons.)

4. Something as simple as *providing help* when a friend needs it is a needed quality in good friendships. We cannot count all the times friends have come to our aid when we needed them. They know we would not call them unless it is important. We value their time. We also know that when

they call us with a cry for help, it is an opportunity for us, not a burden. They respect our problems with time, also.

5. *Being open* is another quality that is necessary in the establishment of a nurturing friendship. However, openness and the establishment of trust go hand in hand. A person does not go about pouring out his innermost thoughts unless he knows his friend can be trusted. Sometimes when there is a feeling that trust is missing, words and openness will not work. In fact, it seems that the more you talk, the worse it gets. These words which seem to go nowhere (there is a feeling of a "hidden agenda") have to be stopped, and the risk taken to deal with the real issue before friends can move to a deeper level of sharing. As stated, this is risky, but there is always some risk in friendships. If a person wants to play it safe and is unwilling to take these and other risks, then the real depth of friendship may never be known. He or she will be safe—but lonely.

People experience openness and trust in relationships in different ways. There are times when we have met someone whom we immediately recognized as having the potential for deep sharing. Martin Marty was perhaps thinking of something similar when he wrote of these friends as persons who have a kind of chemistry that at least at the point of the friendship's birth is a mystery.[65] However, because of something in the person's own experience, this person moves unusually slowly toward openness. It is almost as though we can sense, "This person doesn't trust me as yet." This may become frustrating, because we know that we are trustworthy. It seems like such a waste of time to continue to deal with only safe subjects—the weather, the latest crisis, the football team. However, we cannot demand of another that the person become our trusted friend. We can take the risk first and begin to open up some of the inner recesses of our souls. Since we have already recognized in the person some of the qualities needed for a good friend, the person will probably be an *excellent listener* as we share our depths. If the person continues to refuse to be open with us, and the feeling of trust does not develop, then the friendship will be thwarted in its growth. There must be some equality in the giving and receiving of one another in friendship for growth to take place.

However, once openness and trust are established, there is the need for a constant reminder that a person can only receive meaningfully in friendship what another gives. We may have in our thoughts the description of a "perfect" friend, and how that friend will respond to us. Then we might try to take from our friend what that person does not choose to give. We may eventually learn that you cannot give to yourself by providing a script for a friend to follow. However, if you genuinely give of yourself to a friend, as that person's needs are seen, your friend will in all likelihood search for ways to give creatively to you as a person.

6. Another way of saying the above is that good friendships need the quality of *autonomy of personhood*. You have rights to be yourself. Friends have rights to their personal identities as well. Good open communication and trust will help build the necessary bridges in order for us to find ways to nurture one another at the levels of our differing needs.

7. In the making and keeping of friends, we need to remember the need for a certain *quality of joy*. Gibran describes it this way: "In the sweetness of friendship let there be laughter, and sharing of pleasure."[66] If we picture the qualities of friendships as being only those where deep and heavy subjects are deemed important, we are missing the joy of little things. Friendships need a balance. At times we need to share the deep pains of our souls; at other times we need to experience the intoxication of laughter. Good friends can enjoy sharing an idea that has changed their

lives; equally, pleasure comes in the form of mud and rain and laughter around a flickering campfire.

There is no doubt in our minds that friends are important. They are important to us as individuals; they are important to our families. It is no surprise, then, that we consider the making and keeping of close friends one of the most meaningful challenges life has to offer! It is certainly one significant source of personal and family strength.

7
Building Family Memories—Family Rituals

We had just moved to New York City, where Wallace was to work on his doctorate at Columbia University. An appointment was made with a nearby pediatrician to see our two-month-old son. We made it a family affair by all three of us going. After completing his examination, the pediatrician said, "Now I want you to come into my office because I want to talk with you." Panic! Is something wrong? we wondered anxiously. To our surprise he announced that he wanted to talk with us about our family life. So there in the midst of that vast and impersonal city, and with all the warmth and patience of the proverbial country doctor, he talked with us about keeping our family relationship alive and vital. (He had doubtless observed the wear and tear of graduate school on the marital vitality of many generations of students enrolled in the several schools near his office.) He said there are four important ingredients in a good marriage—love, play, work, and worship. Then he told us of a study in which a group of adults were asked to list childhood memories that they now as adults still remember fondly. In evaluating the data, those doing the study noticed that most memories were of experiences repeated over and over by the family. Our pediatrician called these family traditions. Then he talked with us about building our own family traditions. At that moment, sweet rolls on Sunday morning came to mind!

We were visiting in the home of a friend when on Sunday morning their nine-year-old son proudly announced, "We always have sweet rolls on Sunday morning!" (Of course, that smart mother knew an easy way to get Sunday breakfast.) It was something he could count on. It was pleasant. He looked forward to it. By doing this, the mother was building pleasant family memories out of a family tradition.

In this chapter we want to share with you some thoughts about family rituals because we believe that properly understood and nourished, they can be a source of strength and solidarity in family life. (We will use the terms "family ritual" and "family tradition" interchangeably.) The term "ritual" has been around a long time, but it has mainly belonged to anthropologists and students of religion as they studied other cultures and religious practices. However, in the 1930s a few students of the family began to note that many rituals are also found in the interplay of family relationships. The pioneer family sociologist Willard Waller was perhaps the first to use the term "family rituals" in 1938.[67] Then in the 1940s a pioneering study of family rituals was conducted by James H. S. Bossard and Eleanor Boll which resulted, in 1950, in their classic book *Ritual in Family Living*.[68] Strangely, the subject has hardly been addressed by anyone since that time.

As you read this chapter, we would like you to let your mind wander back to your own childhood to retrieve those traditions, rituals, and memories which even yet across the years rest easy on your mind. (This is doubtless the first time authors have encouraged a wandering mind!) When people are asked to consider their own family rituals, an initial response of many is that they cannot think of any. This is partly because we sometimes associate ritual only with great pomp and circumstance, as at graduation exercises. Erikson identifies a second reason when he notes that it is easier to spot rituals in other cultures (or families) than our own.[69] Our rituals are too close to us to be easily spotted. What appears to be ritual in the lives of other people, often seems like the only logical way of doing things in our own lives. In other words, your behavior appears ritualistic, but mine is plain common sense!

WHAT ARE FAMILY RITUALS?

Bossard and Boll say that a ritual is "a pattern of prescribed formal behavior, pertaining to some specific event, occasion, or situation, which tends to be repeated over and over again."[70] That helps a little. More needs to be said. A trip to the unabridged dictionary to examine the etymology of "rite" may surprise you with the startling information that the word is derived from the Greek *arithmos*. (Now, we know what that means, since we have all studied arithmetic!) That raises a further question as to what a rite or ritual has to do with numbers (the meaning of *arithmos*). Apparently this: just as there is a kind of predictable precision in the science of mathematics, so also there is a predictable precision about the way a ritual is conducted.

This brings us to three unvarying characteristics of a ritual cited by Bossard and Boll.[71] First, *a ritual is prescribed.* Ritual means precision in procedure. You do it this way, not that. For example, most family rituals at Christmas prescribe that the proper way of observing the season requires a decorated tree. In fact, a particular type of tree is prescribed, varying from one part of the country to another, and some family rituals even prescribe when it is put up and taken down. (Wallace's grandmother always took her's, a cedar, down on New Year's Day, burned it and then ate black-eyed peas and hog jowl "to bring good luck all year.")

Secondly, *a ritual is rigid.* That is, it resists change, though it can gradually change under pressure. The longer the tradition has been practiced, the more it resists change. If the tradition was brought over from the Old Country three generations ago, it will resist change much more than if it is only a few years old. When the Catholic leadership a few years ago ruled that the Mass instead of being said in Latin, which had been used for many centuries, should be said in the vernacular, there was great resistance to the change on the part of many faithful Catholics. One elderly lady reported that she just didn't feel as if she had been to Mass now that it was in English!

Thirdly, *as the ritual is repeated over and over, there gradually emerges a sense of rightness about it.* It just seems right to do it this way instead of that way. It may be faster, cheaper, or more efficient to do it another way, but it seems right to do it this way on grounds that are not really logical or rational. Let us use the Christmas season again as an example. When does your family open gifts? Some families open them Christmas Eve, some open them Christmas Day, and some come up with yet a different combination. If you happened to grow up in a family that opened gifts on Christmas morning, it may seem sacrilegious to open them on Christmas Eve! It just seems right to open them Christmas morning. (Isn't that when Jesus opened them?) There is no particular logic to it; it is an emotional matter, and it seems right! Now, if a "Christmas Eve opener" marries a "Christmas morning opener," there is the possibility of real trouble! It is this sense of rightness that distinguishes mere habit from ritual. Also, habit is not accompanied by the ceremony we associate with ritual. However, unless one knows the personal significance of an act to a person, it is difficult to know whether behavior is habit or ritual.

This reminds us that rituals operate on at least two levels: the objective and the subjective.[72] The objective level has to do with the behavior or objects involved in the ritual. For instance, a student reports that in her family her mother baked the bread that the family ate at special meals. It was a practice for her father to begin the meal by breaking the bread by hand as a symbolic act; this was followed by each person taking a piece. At the objective level, this ritual is concerned with bread being broken by the father. At the subjective level, meaning is invested in the act. This meaning has to do with the family's shared life symbolized by eating from the same loaf, and the headship of the man in the family who broke the bread. At the subjective level, the breaking of bread served as a springboard for interpretations and free associations which produced a variety of feelings, emotions, thoughts, and memories in the minds of the participants. It is at this level that the most important part of ritual takes place. The symbolic dimension of ritual reminds us that at times ordinary language and acts are inadequate to express our deepest needs and yearnings.

Ritual and American Culture

Before going further, we want to take recognition of the fact that in many circles the very term "ritual" has bad connotations. In some religious circles (especially nonliturgical churches), one of the most devastating criticisms which can be leveled at a church is that it is "ritualistic." These people interpret ritual to mean empty, mindless, rote behavior during a worship service. Of course, it does not have to be that. Yet even a cursory examination of a "nonritualistic" worship service will reveal a wealth of rituals, if one keeps in mind the three traits of rituals cited earlier.

For instance, a common worship format in these churches permits us to predict that every week worshipers will stand to sing the first hymn and remain standing for a predictable prayer that usually contains some rather predictable phrases. Why don't we sit to sing the first hymn, or at least sit for the prayer? We can also predict that the offering will be taken at a particular point in the service and that we will stand to sing a hymn just before the offering is taken (standing makes it easier to get to the wallet?). The sermon comes at a predictable point, and the service is concluded by the singing of another, but different type of hymn followed by a concluding prayer. In fact, the same benediction may be repeated word for word each week.

If one complains that people in a "ritualistic" church say and do things by rote, it is doubtless equally true that few in the "nonritualistic" churches pay much attention to the words of the hymns they sing or the prayers they utter. In fact, in meaningful rituals, it may not be necessary to pay strict attention to what is being said and done, since the important thing is the mood, the emotional tone established by the total program. Too much consciousness about what is transpiring in a ritual may destroy its power. In some areas of life, we need to "let go and let it happen."

The truth is, Americans are quite ambivalent about ritual. On the one hand, as Margaret Mead observes, we cry out for an opportunity to celebrate, for shared delight, especially among the young; but this need is frustrated by our dislike of anything that is repetitive, ritualistic, familiar.[73] At a deeper level, the celebration and ritual of rock concerts are remarkably similar to the celebration and ritual found in some religious celebrations in parts of Europe and of Central and South America. They also bear strong resemblance to the ecstasy and fervor generated in religious revival meetings. But this antiritual stance is not confined to the United States. British author Robert Bocock asserts that industrial societies in general undervalue the significance and importance of ritual in human welfare.[74]

FUNCTIONS OF FAMILY RITUALS

We began this chapter by saying that we believe a proper understanding and use of family rituals can add strength, solidarity, and satisfaction to contemporary family relationships. It is one way to grow as families. At this point let us examine some functions of ritual in family living.

1. *Through family rituals we transmit cultural values to children.* As noted in Wallace's earlier book, *What's Happening to Our Families?* the traditional functions of the family have largely (but not entirely) been transferred outside the family to factories, offices, and agencies in the community.[75] Among these are the productive, religious, educational, protective, and recreational functions. However, a major function yet residing with the family is that of passing on the culture from one generation to the next. Much of this, though not all, is done through family ritual.[76] By "culture," we refer to the behavior, practices, and values that distinguish people living in one setting from those in another. The family that goes to church or synagogue as a family is by that tradition helping transmit its religious culture to the children. The parent with a bedtime ritual that includes reading to the child is transmitting a cultural value to the child on the importance of reading. The family that gathers around a cake and sings happy birthday is transmitting culture. As the growing child observes and experiences these family rituals over and over, they become deeply engrained.

2. *Rituals bond the family together and contribute to a sense of rootedness.* A major function of ritual, Bocock says, is binding people together.[77] As people share and participate in traditions together, they come to feel a sense of belongingness. As Tevye says in *Fiddler on the Roof*, "Without our traditions, our lives would be shaky, as shaky as a fiddler on a roof." When asked how the fiddlers keep their balance on the roof, he succinctly answers, "Tradition!"[78] There is no doubt that deeply held traditions have a stabilizing effect on us. It helps all of us "fiddlers on the roof" to keep our balance.

For example, I (Wallace) grew up in a family in which everybody sang and played an instrument. I remember well those times when we would gather spontaneously after the evening meal and would sing and play songs, some of which went back generations. (They call it folk music now; we just called it music.) At times the music would seem to take on a life of its own, and we would all be swept up in it in a kind of transcendent experience. Today we would probably say it was a happening. While the singing was satisfying, at a deeper level this shared pleasant experience was bonding us together as a family. We belonged.

Today, we still reenact that tradition in our own family. When our children come home for a visit, we often gather to sing and play instruments. We do so mainly because we enjoy the music. But at a more subtle level, we also do it because an essential genius of ritual is its ability to help us recall past memories and emotions, for as we sing, our bonds as a family are reaffirmed, but we are also rebonded with our past experience and history—our roots.

3. *Family rituals contribute to one's sense of identity.* It is through ritual, Erikson reminds us, that the child comes to develop a sense of corporate identity, of belonging to the larger group.[79] Tevye captures this truth in his opening

monologue to *Fiddler on the Roof* when he tells us that in his Jewish community, the people have traditions for everything—eating, working, dressing. "And because of our traditions," he continues, "everybody knows who he is and what God wants him to do."[80] Their traditions affirmed their identity as Jews. Through our family traditions, we affirm our identities as a Kirby or a Wayne.

Through family rituals, one develops not only corporate identity but personal identity as well. (Of course, you cannot always make neat distinctions between corporate and personal identity.) Religious rituals help the child to think of himself or herself as a Baptist, a Methodist, a Catholic. For me (Juanita), this belonging to a larger group, in my case a "church family," was the source of many traditions in my youth. It was with this church family that I have so many memories surrounding Christmas and New Year celebrations, church picnics and banquets, all of which contributed to my sense of identity and rootedness. The affirmation I received from this "family" for speaking to a group or performing on a musical instrument helped me to feel competent and valued as a person.

Some rituals communicate something about the status and identity of other family members. "That's your father's chair," tells the child something about Father's position. Erikson notes that the rather ritualized dimensions of the way a mother cares for her infant not only help form a bond between mother and child but also confirm her identity as a mother.[81]

The point being made here is that through family rituals, we are often taught something about our identities—Denton or Holt, as competent or incompetent, as an athlete, musician, or scholar, as Protestant or Catholic, as male or female.

4. *Rituals give predictability and order to family life.* We have

already noted that a major characteristic of a ritual is that of prescription. This prescription imparts predictability and structure to life. In the classic book, *The Little Prince*, the fox captured this truth when teaching the little prince the importance of "proper rites." Because of proper rites, the fox noted that he could predict that on Thursdays those who usually hunted him would instead spend the day dancing with the village girls. He therefore had no need to fear and could roam freely through the countryside. "But if the hunters danced at just any time," he told the little prince, "every day would be like every other day, and I should never have any vacation at all."[82]

Because much of the routine of daily family living becomes ritualized, structure is imparted to family life and reduces stress. For example, use of the bathroom in the morning is a critical issue where several people must use the one available bathroom. (During the writing of this book, we were reminded of this truth in the small apartment in which we lived on a sabbatical. When our children visited us, we had to juggle schedules—and degrees of urgency—in order to use the one small bathroom.) One student reports that in her family the father always got up first and used the bathroom. Then the mother used it, followed by each child according to age. This bathroom ritual gave some order and predictability and reduced stress in what otherwise could become a chaotic situation. Even the ritual of each person sitting in the same chair at mealtime makes for a smoother-running family. No decisions have to be made about this at each meal. A certain amount of ritualization of family life also takes place in meal preparation, doing the laundry, dishwashing, bathing, and bedtime routines, all of which impart a measure of predictability.

5. *Family ritual provides for the renewal of celebration.* To quote the fox again, rites are "what makes one day different

from other days, and one hour from other hours."[83] Family rituals and traditions break the routine of life; they give us something to look forward to, and provide us with an opportunity to renew our sense of celebration. A major appeal of family rituals is the anticipation of joy they bring. Because of past birthday celebrations, the forthcoming birthday is all the more eagerly anticipated by the child. With the approach of Christmas and its attendant rituals, life takes on a new sense of zest, people seem friendlier, and some of our students say that even tough professors are a bit more understanding. Why? Perhaps it is the anticipation of the renewal of high emotions associated with the holiday.

For a celebration to be most meaningful, it must have something in it for the whole family. This may be why Christmas continues to bring delight and joy to so many people. The youngest child senses the excitement and is fascinated by the array of colors and lights; the older child has "visions of sugarplums" dancing in his head; the teenager remembers childhood Christmases when she was yet innocent and has some vague sense of regret over the loss of that innocence; parents relive their childhoods as they remember their own parents and Christmases as a family; grandparents feel awed by the changes that have taken place since they were young, and yet there is a continuity even in the midst of change because many songs they sing are songs they sang as children. All of this is further enhanced by it being a communitywide, nationwide celebration. Everyone shares the joy of the occasion.

CHILDREN AND FAMILY RITUALS

Because of the affinity of children for rituals and the pivotal role they play in each child's development, the subject deserves special attention. Early in his career the eminent psychologist Jean Piaget observed that children's behavior, especially their play, becomes ritualized.[84] Anyone with children is aware that a child rather early falls into the routine of family life in such a way that he or she is immensely distressed by any deviation from the routine. This reaches a peak at about age two and a half. At this age, Gesell and Ilg note, the child has a "very strong ritualistic sense of having everything at home in its usual place and done in its usual way."[85] Woe unto the father who happens to sit in his wife's usual chair at the mealtable! The small child is so distressed by this variation of family routine that a major ruckus is raised and seating has to be changed before the meal can proceed. Why does the child have this intense need for everything to be done according to the usual routine? The likely answer lies in the child's sense of helplessness on the one hand and the predictability of rituals on the other hand. By age two and a half, the child has become increasingly aware of the environment and yet has so little control over that environment. Parents and older sibs control that. Bossard and Boll speculate that the "rhythmic repetition of intimate family acts" (such as predicting who will sit where) impart to the child a sense of confidence and security.[86]

As the children grow older, they continue to have a need for and enjoy family rituals (as indeed we do throughout life), but the rigidity and intensity of this need peaks in early childhood. Of course, many agencies and commercial enterprises are aware of and capitalize on the need of children for ritual. In the heyday of television's *Mickey Mouse Club*, our son was too small to appreciate most of the program, but he did like the ritualized opening which always began with the same song and dance. He would eagerly crawl into the room and watch the opening, then promptly lose interest after the ritualized part was over.

One appeal of groups such as Boy Scouts and Girl Scouts is the ritualized opening and closing ceremonies. Public schools used to begin classes each day with a ritualized opening that included the Pledge of Allegiance to the Flag. Ritual is now largely confined to sporting events where the group is led by cheerleaders in ritualistic yells, some of which threaten mayhem to the opposition (sock 'em, bust 'em, bend 'em, twist 'em).

We believe that parents need to become more aware of and take advantage of children's affinity for ritual. Bedtime rituals often make it easier to get the child to bed at night. Rituals are particularly important in the child's religious training. The major part of our religious heritage which we take from childhood into adulthood is that part of our religious education which was repetitively experienced, i.e., ritualized. This includes regular and predictable attendance at church by the family, attendance at Sunday school, asking the blessing at mealtime, and perhaps some form of family worship such as family Bible-reading or saying the Rosary together. The specific content of a sermon is usually soon forgotten. But the cumulative effect of regular worship attendance as a family (especially when church is a pleasant experience) engraves lasting impressions on the attitudes and values of a child, values that are not easily forgotten in adulthood. In his autobiography, Albert Schweitzer says that one of the main things his parents did for him was to take him to worship services, even though he was too young to understand much. But he says it is not important that children understand everything; what is important is "that they shall feel something of what is serious and solemn." He continues, "The fact that the child sees his elders full of devotion, and has to feel something of devotion himself, that is what gives the service meaning for him."[87] A ritual that appears to the child to be taken seriously by the adults and is reinforced by their lifestyle is a powerful medium for teaching.

Toward Developing Your Family Rituals

In this section of the chapter we are primarily concerned with rituals of celebration that may have come from the previous generation or perhaps have developed out of your interactions together as a family. Traditions that have been inherited are often more elaborate by virtue of the fact that they are older. Rituals generated within the immediate family are less complex.

1. *Nourish meaningful family traditions inherited from your families.* What traditions do you remember your family as observing? The way in which holidays and anniversaries were celebrated will come to mind immediately. Perhaps some traditions have been abandoned or halfheartedly observed which could be profitably dusted off and updated. Perhaps a special dish was cooked for certain occasions. Others may remember when the family would gather for a homecoming and could reinstitute that tradition.

At this point we are emphasizing those traditions which have a history behind them. This reflects our belief that the older the tradition, the greater its potential for nourishing our lives. In reenacting the tradition, we are joined with our forefathers in celebrating life, and thereby develop roots which we in our rootless, industrial society so desperately need.

A danger with old traditions is that the symbolism in them has become so archaic or so elaborate that the contemporary person is either unable to identify with the symbolism, or is overwhelmed with the elaborateness of the ritual. Thus, modern families walk a fine line between, on the one hand, finding old traditions so out of date or elaborate that they are meaningless, and, on the other hand, destroying the value of the traditions' age if many changes are made.

2. *Encourage meaningful family rituals which have developed in your family.* Some rituals are inherited; others are unique to your family. An examination of your family life will doubtless uncover some that have developed rather spontaneously. You didn't plan them, but there they are. For example, we never planned to make a ritual of going to the local Annual Book Fair with the children. But for over a dozen years Juanita and the children have attended it, which in retrospect is one of our treasured traditions, and one still observed. Another couple noticed that they had developed a ritual of occasionally eating after the children were asleep. At these special times they sat on pillows around a coffee table and by candlelight had a romantic meal together.

Every family has rituals in undeveloped forms which can, by a little attention, be fanned into the flame of meaningful experiences.

3. *Consciously develop new rituals for your family.* In his classic 1910 study of rituals, Frederick Henke observes that one way rituals come into existence is by consciously developing them.[88] For instance, you may want to introduce a bedtime ritual if you have children in the home. In one of our groups a couple shared a ritual they have where, in alternate months, the husband and then the wife secretly plans a special night out. Another couple liked the idea so much, they adopted the practice for themselves. Try new ideas. Then modify them as seems appropriate.

5. *Let family rituals grow up with the family.* To insist that a ritual be observed exactly the same way throughout the lifetime of the family is potentially disastrous. For instance, bedtime prayers with your child at age six are one thing. To

insist on bedtime prayers ten years later will likely get you thrown out of the room! If rituals are to continue to be meaningful, they must be able to be adapted and changed with changing circumstances in the family. In this case, old outgrown rituals need to be modified or replaced with those more suited to the family's needs today.

We developed a bedtime ritual when our son was less than a year old. As practiced then, it called for me (Wallace) to give him his nightly bath and get him dressed for bed (all carefully engineered by Juanita). I then read and/or sang nursery rhymes to him. Then holding him in my arms, I repeated the same formula to him every night, "Now then, Son, I want you to know that I love you, Mother loves you, and God loves you. Amen." This was modified when our daughter was born and further modified as the children grew older, though the same basic formula was used for a number of years. It was finally discontinued when it became apparent that they were too old for bedtime rituals.

What we have been saying throughout the pages of this book is that if through family rituals and intimacy, and friendships, and rules, and all that we have written about; if these help children to know that they are loved and wanted; if teenagers can be reassured that they are loved and belong; if adults can be loved and affirmed; if the elderly can be confirmed as loved and respected members of the family, then these ingredients of healthy families shall have made important contributions to the growth and integration of that family. We remind you again: You don't have to have a sick family for it to be made better!

Appendix:
Questions and Exercises

Chapter 1
Growth Through Personal Identity

1. Centuries ago, families in Europe often had coats of arms which in visual form told something of the history of the family, its victories, etc. Sometimes a family motto was emblazoned on the coat of arms, such as, "One for all and all for one." On a large piece of paper, you and your mate draw your own special coat of arms. Be sure to include important events and people so that the story of your lives is told. What is your family motto? You might want to hang this "work of art" in your home. If you are doing this with other couples, take three or four minutes to explain your coats of arms to other couples.

2. Share with your mate two or three ways your family background has influenced your idea of what it means to be a woman (man), wife (husband), mother (father).

Chapter 2
Portrait of Strong, Healthy Families

1. Below are the eight qualities we discussed as characterizing healthy, strong families. Consider each one; then

rate your family on each by putting a check in the proper box.

Healthy Family Characteristic	Work Badly Needed	Could Use Work	About Average	Above Average	Strong Point
1. Good communication					
2. Open expression of feelings					
3. Effective crisis management					
4. Structure without rigidity					
5. Strong family bonds, loyalty, identity					
6. Respect for child's individuality					
7. Clear parental leadership					
8. Much affirmation of each other					

2. What might *you* do to improve your score on the weakest points above?

3. What might your mate do to improve on your weakest scores?

4. What might your children do to help improve your weakest scores?

5. Since good communication seems to characterize all healthy families, complete the following and then share with your mate:

a. I have trouble communicating with you when I think you . . .

b. Sometimes I am afraid to be open with you about my feelings because . . .

c. The area of our relationship that I would most like to talk with you about is . . .

d. One thing I could do to improve our communication is . . .

Chapter 3
Enriching Your Sexual Relationship

Complete this form and then share answers with your mate using this as a basis for your discussion.

1. I would like to talk with you about the following areas of our sexual relationship. Circle as many as needed.

a. frequency
b. taking initiative
c. positions
d. touching
e. contraceptives
f. foreplay
g. afterplay
h. what turns me off
i. noise—bed, child
j. romance, gentleness
k. distractions
l. bed clothes (on or off?)
m. lighting (on or off?)
n. covers (up or down?)

o. time to be alone
p. what turns me on
q. possible pregnancy
r. "You're only nice in bed."
s. feeling pushed away
t. feeling pushed into
u. oral sex
v. more variety
w. timing
x. talking—before, during, after
y. signals of readiness
z. relationships outside the bedroom

2. The one above that I would like most to talk with you about is . . .

3. One area I would like to talk with you about that is *not* listed above is . . .

4. The area that I find most difficult to talk with you about is . . .

5. You could help me talk more comfortably about our sexual relationship if you would . . .

6. I am afraid to talk with you about our sexual relationship for fear you will . . .

Chapter 4
Guidelines for Living with Children

1. Reflect on what you consider to be the five most important qualities a person needs to be a good parent. Then give your parents a grade (A, B, C, D, F) on each point; then grade yourself. (No cheating!)

Appendix: Questions and Exercises

Important Parental Quality	My Mother	My Father	My Self
1.			
2.			
3.			
4.			
5.			

2. In what ways do you see yourself doing things with your children that you learned from your parents which you like and want to reaffirm?

3. In what ways do you sometimes see yourself making the same mistakes rearing your children that your parents made with you? What can you do about it?

4. What are the big issues in your family regarding rearing children (which may or may not be mentioned above)? Discuss these with your mate. Agree to do one thing that might help the situation.

5. Take a piece of paper and draw a large circle covering most of the sheet to represent your family. Now, tell a story about your family *as you perceive it* by drawing circles

(females) and squares (males) inside the larger circle. (Yes, the children can do this.)

   a. The size of the circle or square should indicate the relative power or influence each family member has. Thus, a four-year-old might have a larger circle or square than a ten-year-old. The person who "quarterbacks" the family will have the largest circle or square.

   b. The distance each circle or square is from others indicates who seems to relate most closely to others. (This is different from who loves whom the most.) If Junior is very close to Mother, you might overlap very significantly his square with Mother's circle. If Dad is a remote figure in the family, put him away from the others. After you have finished your project, discuss it with other family members. Also explain how you would like it to be different. You are to listen while others explain. No one criticizes or belittles another's perception of the family.

Chapter 5
Relating to the Other Generation

1. List two or three positive ways in which in-laws have enriched your lives.

2. Consider one thing that you can do to affirm your in-laws for ways they have enriched your lives.

3. What are two or three ways in which in-laws create stress or conflict in your lives?

4. Consider one thing that you might do to gently, but firmly, deal with your in-laws so as to reduce the stress. (As a general guideline, we think it is best for *you* to deal with your relative, i.e., for the husband to deal with his, say,

mother even though it is his wife who is most upset by the mother's behavior.)

5. In order to help you develop some understanding for the other generation (in-laws or aging parents), and possibly find solutions to problems, do a role play with your mate. For instance, suppose your father-in-law tries to give you too much advice and this is a real problem for you. One of you play his part, and the other try out different responses to him. First, you might say exactly what you'd like to say. Then try out gentler, but direct responses. Then let the other person be the father-in-law. Also try to "stand in his shoes" and tell why giving this advice is important to him (he feels needed, etc.). After doing the role play, discuss with each other what you learned out of the experience. How did you feel while playing the other's role? Does any of this suggest a new course of action?

6. What have you done for your aging parent lately (or perhaps one who is middle-aged) which would communicate caring and affirmation? How long has it been since you expressed appreciation to your father or mother for the positive things he or she has contributed to your life? (No need to mention the negative contributions at this time.) What else might you do to indicate care for them?

Chapter 6
Friendship: Source of Personal and Family Strength

1. Think of someone whom you consider the type of person who makes a good friend. List five qualities this person has that lead you to think he or she would make a good friend. Then rate yourself on these qualities.

Friend's Qualities	I need to improve 1	2	One of my strong points 3	4	5
1.					
2.					
3.					
4.					
5.					

2. Below are some qualities often associated with a good friend. Rate yourself on each one by putting a 1 there if you do poorly in that area, or a 5 if this is one of your stronger points. Leave it blank if it seems unimportant to you.

____ trustworthy
____ doesn't criticize
____ similar interest
____ listens to me
____ interested in me
____ likes me
____ stimulates my thinking
____ is friendly

____ accepts me
____ even-tempered
____ good conversationalist
____ willing to help me
____ expresses appreciation
____ suggests doing things
____ likes to be with me

3. Make a list of five persons whom you consider to be close family friends. Then consider the following:
   a. What have you done together in the last month or two?
   b. Was your mate included in whatever you have done together?
   c. Have your children been included in these activities?
   d. In each instance, put a G if you were the primary giver in these activities (how did you give?), an R if you were primarily a receiver, and an E if you and your friend both gave equally.

Now, evaluate the above. What do these tell you about your friendships? Does it throw any light on the kind of friend you happen to be?

Chapter 7
Building Family Memories—Family Rituals

1. Consider some of the rituals (traditions) which you see your family as having in each of the following categories. Children can also join in on this one.

   a. holidays   e. seasons
   b. mealtime   f. work
   c. anniversaries   g. bedtime
   d. birthdays   h. worship

Add any others that occur to you. Which rituals bring the greatest satisfaction? Which rituals cause the greatest stress (indicating a need for readjustment)? Which ritual needs to be encouraged and developed? Can you think of an area in which you might develop a meaningful new ritual?

2. What rituals does your family have that you "inherited" from your parents?

3. Reflect back on your childhood home. What family rituals did you have then which, even today, still leave pleasant memories? Share these with your mate (or the group, if you are doing this with a group).

Notes

1. Erik Erikson, *Identity and the Life Cycle* (W. W. Norton & Co., 1980), p. 101.
2. Daniel Levinson, *The Seasons of a Man's Life* (Ballantine Books, 1978), p. 109.
3. Abraham Maslow, *Toward a Psychology of Being* (D. Van Nostrand Co., 1968), p. 5.
4. Donald Price, "Normal, Functional, and Unhealthy," *Family Coordinator*, 28:109–114 (Jan. 1979).
5. John S. Sennott, "Healthy Family Functioning Scale: Family Members' Perceptions of Cohesion, Adaptability, and Communication," unpublished doctoral dissertation (Purdue University, May 1981), p. 17.
6. Douglas Sprenkle, David Olson, "Circumplex Model of Marital and Family Systems: An Empirical Study of Clinic and Non-clinic Couples," *Journal of Marriage and Family Counseling*, 4:59–74 (April 1978).

David Olson, Douglas Sprenkle, Candyce Russell, "Circumplex Model of Marital and Family Systems: I. Cohesion and Adaptability Dimensions, Family Types and Clinical Applications," *Family Process*, 18:3–28 (March 1979).

David Olson, Candyce Russell, Douglas Sprenkle, "Circumplex Model of Marital and Family Systems: II. Empirical Studies and Clinical Intervention," in J. Vincent (ed.), *Advances in Family Intervention Assessment and Theory*, Vol. 1 (JAI Press, 1980), pp. 129–176.

7. Michael Warner, Concordia Theological Seminary, Ft.

Wayne, Indiana. Personal conversation with Wallace Denton.

8. George Bach and Peter Wyden, *The Intimate Enemy* (Avon Books, 1968).

9. Olson, Russell, Sprenkle, in Vincent (ed.), *Advances in Family Intervention Assessment and Theory*, p. 131.

10. Nick Stinnett, "In Search of Strong Families," in N. Stinnett and others (eds.), *Building Family Strengths* (University of Nebraska Press, 1979), p. 26.

11. Myron Madden, *The Power to Bless* (Broadman Press, 1979).

12. Willard Waller and Reuben Hill, *The Family: A Dynamic Interpretation* (Dryden Press, 1959), p. 58.

13. Tom F. Driver, "On Taking Sex Seriously," *Christianity and Crisis*, Oct. 14, 1962, p. 177.

14. Oliver Spurgeon English and Gerald H. J. Pearson, *Emotional Problems of Living*, rev. ed. (W. W. Norton & Co., 1955), p. 402.

15. William Graham Cole, *Sex in Christianity and Psychoanalysis* (Oxford University Press, 1955).

16. Howard Gadlin, "A Critical View of the History of Intimate Relations in the United States," in George Levinger and Harold Rauch (eds.), *Close Relationships* (University of Massachusetts Press, 1977), p. 67.

17. Alfred Kinsey et al., *Sexual Behavior in the Human Female* (W. B. Saunders Co., 1953), p. 427.

18. Wallace Denton, *Family Problems and What to Do About Them* (Westminster Press, 1971), Ch. 6, "Avoiding the Dry Rot in Marriage."

19. John Levy and Ruth L. Monroe, *The Happy Family* (Alfred A. Knopf, 1938), p. 45.

20. Raul Schiavi, cited in Sue Millar, "Why Your Sex Drive May Suddenly Wane: What You Can Do About It," *Glamour*, Oct. 1981, p. 263.

21. Max Lerner, *America as a Civilization* (Simon & Schuster, 1957), p. 562.

22. Alice Rossi, "Transitions of Parenthood," *Journal of Marriage and the Family*, 30:26–39 (Feb. 1968).

23. Howard and Charlotte Clinebell, *The Intimate Marriage* (Harper & Row, 1970), p. 118.

24. Dorothy Briggs, *Your Child's Self-Esteem* (Doubleday & Co., 1975), p. 47.

Notes

25. Abraham Maslow, *Motivation and Personality* (Harper & Row, 1954).
26. Erik Erikson, *Childhood and Society* (W. W. Norton & Co., 1950), p. 249.
27. Stanley Coopersmith, *The Antecedents of Self-Esteem* (W. H. Freeman Co., 1967), p. 236.
28. Evelyn M. Duvall, *Marriage and Family Development*, 4th ed. (J. B. Lippincott Co., 1979), p. 297.
29. Sam Keen, *To a Dancing God* (Harper & Row, 1970), p. 100.
30. Virginia Satir, *Peoplemaking* (Science and Behavior Books, 1972), p. 211.
31. Judson T. Landis and Mary G. Landis, *Building a Successful Marriage*, 7th ed. (Prentice-Hall, 1977), p. 290.
32. Ibid.
33. Ibid., p. 291.
34. Robert Blood and Donald Wolfe, *Husbands and Wives* (Free Press, 1960), p. 248.
35. Howard Hovde, *The Neo-Married* (Judson Press, 1968), p. 48.
36. Margaret Mead, "The Contemporary American Family as an Anthropologist Sees It," *American Journal of Sociology*, 53:453–459 (May 1948).
37. Landis and Landis, *Building a Successful Marriage*, p. 297.
38. Eda LeShan, *The Wonderful Crisis of Middle Age* (Warner Paperback Library, 1973), p. 223.
39. Gail Sheehy, *Passages* (E. P. Dutton & Co., 1974), p. 65.
40. Erik Erikson, *Gandhi's Truth* (W. W. Norton & Co., 1969), p. 395.
41. Robert Coles, *Erik Erikson: The Growth of His Work* (Little Brown & Co., 1970), p. 274.
42. Dorothy B. Fritz, *Growing Old Is a Family Affair* (John Knox Press, 1972), p. 7.
43. Paul Tournier, *Learning to Grow Old* (SCM Press, 1971), p. 72.
44. Fritz, *Growing Old Is a Family Affair*, p. 16.
45. Barbara Silverstone and Helen K. Hyman, *You and Your Aging Parent* (Pantheon Books, 1976), p. 66.
46. Andrew D. Lester and Judith L. Lester, *Understanding Aging Parents* (Westminster Press, 1980), p. 28.
47. Silverstone and Hyman, *You and Your Aging Parent*, p. 55.

48. Ibid., p. 138.
49. Carle C. Zimmerman and Lucius Cervantes, *Successful American Families* (Pageant Press, 1960), p. 14.
50. C. S. Lewis, *The Four Loves* (Harcourt, Brace & Co., 1960), p. 83.
51. Ibid., p. 80.
52. William Schofield, *Psychotherapy: The Purchase of Friendship* (Prentice-Hall, 1964), p. 162.
53. Antoine de Saint-Exupéry, *The Little Prince*, tr. by Katherine Woods (Reynal & Hitchcock, 1943), pp. 66, 67.
54. Hugh Black, *Friendship* (Fleming H. Revell, 1898), p. 41.
55. Joel D. Block, *Friendship: How to Give It, How to Get It* (Macmillan Publishing Co., 1980), p. 41.
56. Martin Marty, *Friendship* (Argus Communications, 1980), p. 171.
57. Paul Tournier, *To Understand Each Other* (John Knox Press, 1962), p. 29.
58. Margaret Sawin, *Family Enrichment with Family Clusters* (Judson Press, 1979), p. 26.
59. Zimmerman and Cervantes, *Successful American Families*, p. 170.
60. Kahlil Gibran, *The Prophet* (Alfred A. Knopf, 1923), p. 65.
61. Theodor Reik, *Listening with the Third Ear* (Farrar, Straus & Co., 1948), p. 513.
62. Zimmerman and Cervantes, *Successful American Families*, p. 170.
63. Marty, *Friendship*, p. 63.
64. de Saint-Exupéry, *The Little Prince*, p. 67.
65. Marty, *Friendship*, p. 33
66. Gibran, *The Prophet*, p. 65.
67. Willard Waller, *The Family: A Dynamic Interpretation* (Cordon Co., 1938).
68. James H. S. Bossard and Eleanor Boll, *Ritual in Family Living* (University of Pennsylvania Press, 1950).
69. Erik Erikson, *Toys and Reasons* (W. W. Norton & Co., 1977), p. 80.
70. Bossard and Boll, *Ritual in Family Living*, p. 9.
71. Ibid., p. 16.
72. Paul Jones, *Recovering Ritual* (Paulist/Newman Press, 1973), p. 4

Notes

73. Margaret Mead, *Twentieth Century Faith: Hope and Survival* (Harper & Row, 1972), p. 124.
74. Robert Bocock, *Ritual in Industrial Society* (London: George Allen & Unwin, 1974), p. 24.
75. Wallace Denton, *What's Happening to Our Families?* (Westminster Press, 1964), pp. 28–39.
76. Bossard and Boll, *Ritual in Family Living*, p. 39
77. Bocock, *Ritual in Industrial Society*, p. 9.
78. Joseph Stein, *Fiddler on the Roof* (Crown Publishers, 1964), p. 1.
79. Erikson, *Toys and Reasons*, p. 79.
80. Stein, *Fiddler on the Roof*, p. 1.
81. Erikson, *Toys and Reasons*, p. 87.
82. de Saint-Exupéry, *The Little Prince*, p. 68.
83. Ibid.
84. Jean Piaget, *Play, Dreams and Imitation in Childhood*, tr. by C. Cattegno and F. M. Hodgson (W. W. Norton & Co., 1962), pp. 92–93.
85. Arnold L. Gesell and Frances Ilg, *The Child from Five to Ten* (Harper & Brothers, 1946), p. 347.
86. Bossard and Boll, *Ritual in Family Living*, p. 35.
87. Albert Schweitzer, *Memoirs of Childhood and Youth* (Macmillan Co., 1931), p. 62.
88. Frederick Henke, *A Study in the Psychology of Ritualism* (University of Chicago Press, 1910), pp. 39–40.